STAIRWAY TO SUCCESS

Nido R. Qubein

Stairway to Success

Creative Services, Inc.
806 Westchester Drive, P.O. Box 6008
High Point, NC 27262 USA
Phone: 336-889-3010
Fax: 336-885-3001
www.NidoQubein.com

Published by   **Executive Books**
206 West Allen Street
Mechanicsburg, PA 17055

Printed in the United States of America

ISBN: 0-937539-67-8 (Paperback)
      0-937539-66-X (Hardcover)

ALSO BY NIDO QUBEIN

ACHIEVING PEAK PERFORMANCE

HOW TO BE A GREAT COMMUNICATOR

HOW TO GET ANYTHING YOU WANT

COMMUNICATE LIKE A PRO

HOW TO BE A GREAT SALES PROFESSIONAL

HOW TO SELL, SERVE AND SUCCEED

HOW TO POSITION YOURSELF FOR SUCCESS

MARKETING PROFESSIONAL SERVICES

THE CRESTCOM MANAGEMENT SERIES

THE TIME IS NOW, THE PERSON IS YOU

To Michael,
with love.

ACKNOWLEDGMENTS

My life has been an incredible blessing. And I owe it all to my God, my family, and my friends. I express gratitude and deep appreciation:

To my hometown folks in High Point, North Carolina.

To the generous members of the Nido Qubein Associates Scholarship Foundation who, since 1972, have helped to educate over 300 deserving young people.

To my fellow professionals in the National Speakers Association.

To my talented associates in Speakers Roundtable.

To my dedicated staff at Creative Services.

To the executives I've served with on many corporate, university, and community boards of directors.

To the thousands of audiences I've been fortunate to share with over the years, and the wonderful speaker bureaus who got me there.

To Mount Olive College, High Point University, American Humanics Foundation, Sales and Marketing International, The United Way, and so many more who were kind to bestow upon me various awards and honors.

And especially to the United States of America for granting me the privilege of becoming a naturalized citizen and pursuing my dreams as a productive entrepreneur.

Thank you.

TABLE OF CONTENTS

Stairway To Success

The Complete Blueprint for Personal and Professional Achievement

Introduction

They can because they think they can.

— Virgil

Wherever my career takes me — from my home town of High Point, North Carolina to the min-istate of Luxembourg; from the island city-state of Singapore to the island continent of Australia — I encounter people pursuing a common quest: success.

Many come to me in search of a secret formula. They've labored for years, butted their heads against walls, suffered failure and rejection, and still they wonder: "Is it possible for me to achieve success, given my level of talent and education?"

And I have a ready response: *You can if you want to*.

Success is not a matter of luck, an accident of birth, or a reward for virtue. It is a matter of *decision, commitment, planning, preparation, execution,* and *recommitment.* Success doesn't come to you; you must go to it. The trail is well-traveled and well marked. If you want to walk it, you can. This book will help you find the right steps.

"But you've got to have talent to be successful," people tell me, and they're right.

But everyone has talent.

Michael Jordan's talent is bouncing a basketball down the court and plopping it through a round hoop. That's how he made it to superstardom. When he tried swinging a baseball bat and catching a baseball with a leather glove, they sent him down to the minors.

Henry Ford's talent was building automobiles. He wouldn't have made it as the CEO of an insurance company, and he was far from brilliant as the CEO of an automobile company. But when it came to the manufacturing process, his talent shone.

Richard Burton's talent was acting. He was an indifferent singer. When he starred in "Camelot," the musical burden was carried by the likes of Julie Andrews and Robert Goulet. But Burton excelled at acting the role of King Arthur.

Some people are talented at driving nails, some at shaping clay, some at speaking before audiences, some at writing novels, some at skating, some at dancing, some at sewing, some at cooking.

But everyone is talented. We're just talented in different ways. If you want to succeed, identify the areas in which you are talented and commit to developing those talents to the fullest.

You can do it if you want to. The secret is in the six steps I'll outline in this book:

Step 1.   *Decision.* Decide what you want in life. Make it a decision that comes from deep inside you. This means getting to know yourself. Identify the things you do well and the things you enjoy doing. Get familiar with the way you respond to your environment and why you respond that way. Learn where you're strong and play to your strengths. When you've defined yourself, you can also define the success you want — and can begin the journey toward your dreams..

Step 2.   *Commitment.* It's one thing to decide what you want. It's another thing to make a commitment. A commitment is like your signature on a contract: It binds you to a course of action. When you make a deep commitment to a goal, powerful forces come into play, propelling you toward that goal. The power comes from within you. It's there, and you may not even know it.

Step 3.   *Planning.* Here is where one three-letter word separates losers from winners. That word is *How.* Losers ask "Can I do it?" Winners ask "How can I do it?" Losers are guided by what's impossible. They see barriers and they stop in their tracks. Winners are guided by what's possible. They see possibilities and then build upon them. By devising a strategy one possibility at a time, they achieve their goals.

Step 4   *Preparation.* Once you know where you want to go, your next step is to prepare yourself for the journey. Preparation involves acquiring the physical, mental/emotional, social and spiritual balance you'll need to keep yourself on course, and the motivation to provide you with the energy to carry it out.

Step 5.   *Execution.* Executing your life's plan involves three phases: Action, learning and applying. A good coach knows that a brilliant game plan is no good without proper execution. The team has to *act* upon the plan. It's the same with your success plan. It's not enough to have one. You have to implement it through positive action. Coupled with the action must be a learning process that allows you to profit from your inevitable mistakes. We never know whether a specific action will be successful until we've tried it. Once we've tried it, we can observe the results, learning what works and what doesn't. Winners expect to make mistakes, but they use them as lessons. They apply what they learn toward implementation of the plan.

Step 6. *Recommitment.* When you've achieved the last goal in your action plan, don't stop. Your life is not at an end. You're at a new beginning — unless you plan to die as soon as your vision is fulfilled. Successful people know that life is a continuously unfolding process, and they remain in control of the unfolding. When they reach that long-sought plateau, they immediately create their next vision. They move on to new plateaus, making new decisions and new commitments, planning, preparing and executing until the new vision is achieved. Success builds upon success.

If you follow these six steps, you'll succeed — not because there's magic in the formula but because there's power in you — the power to accomplish whatever you want to accomplish. And with God's help, you can do it.

Stairway To Success

Prelude to Step One

What Do You Want To Do?

Decision is the spark that ignites action. Until a decision is made, nothing happens.

–Wilfred A. Peterson

The road to success begins with the question: What do you want to do?

You've heard that question often. You come home Friday evening and your spouse asks, "What do you want to do this weekend?" and you shrug and say, "I don't know. What do *you* want to do?"

And since neither of you is willing to make a decision, you end up doing nothing in particular. Before you know it, it's Monday again and all you've accomplished is getting the Sunday paper read.

You heard the question when you were in high school. Maybe you were on summer break, and your best friend asked: "Whatta you wanna do?" and you shrugged and said, "I dunno. Whatta *you* wanna do?" and because neither of you came up with an answer you spent the summer goofing off. Soon it was time to go back to school and you had little to show for the summer, except perhaps a sunburn.

Many people let their early adulthood slip away in just this way. They party through their 20s, drifting from one good time to another, never really answering the question, "What do you want to do?" Then suddenly they're facing their 30th birthday, or their 35th or their 40th. They begin to feel the weight of responsibility. They know they can't keep drifting through life. They have families, mortgages and orthodontist's bills. They have to do something with their lives. But what?

The earlier you confront that question, the better, but it's never too late. At whatever age you find yourself, you can decide what you want to do with the rest of your life, and you can begin doing it. The first step is the decision.

If you're a young person, don't think that you have to give up the joys of youth for the rigors of work and study. Success is not an either/or proposition: either work or pleasure; either the party or the grindstone. Success consists of finding a happy balance between work and pleasure. In fact, truly successful people make their work a *part* of their pleasure. They decide what they want from life, and they choose their careers in harmony with those decisions. They base their career choices on what they enjoy doing, not on what they *have* to do.

What is success?

That's a question you have to answer for yourself. No one else can define success for you. Luciano Pavarotti's mother wanted him to become a banker. But that wasn't Pavarotti's definition of success. He wrote his own definition and became what he wanted to be: a great operatic tenor.

For Donald Trump, success meant making lots of money. For Ted Turner, it meant building a media empire that could challenge the major networks. For Albert Einstein it meant unraveling the secrets of the universe. For Henry Aaron it meant surpassing Babe Ruth's record of 714 lifetime home runs. For Mother Theresa it meant ministering to the needs of the destitute in India.

What will it take to make *you* feel successful?

You won't really succeed unless the things you accomplish bring you pleasure and satisfaction. What good would it do you to win an all-expense-paid Caribbean cruise if you hated sunshine and water and were terrified of ships?

How satisfying would it be for you to be nominated for a seat in your state legislature if you hated politics?

How excited would you be over a promotion to sales manager if your real interests lay in research and development?

So you begin your climb to success by deciding what success means for you.

You lay the foundation for that decision by asking three questions:

(1) What am I good at?
(2) What do I enjoy doing?
(3) What values are important to me?

When you identify something that you do well, that you enjoy doing, and that supports the values that are important to you, you have defined success in your terms.

Chapter One

What Are You Good At?

The crowning fortune of a person is to be born to some pursuit which finds them employment and happiness. Whether it be to make baskets, or broadswords, or canals, or statues or songs.

— Ralph Waldo Emerson.

Success will come easier when you're doing the things you do well. That's obvious.

But many people go through life without giving serious thought to what they really do well. I've known talented writers who lived out their lives as clerical workers, never considering that they might find rewarding careers as novelists or in journalism, public relations or advertising. I've known people who were animated and articulate who spent their lives as cab drivers when their talents might have carried them into television news or some other exciting communications career. I've known people with minds like calculators who spent their lives on assembly lines instead of in finance departments. I've known people who could paint lifelike portraits, but who spent their days behind sales counters instead of in front of easels.

There's nothing wrong with being a clerical worker, or assembly-line worker or a cab driver or a sales clerk, if that's what you like to do and it's what you do well. But too many people drift into these jobs because they were the first things available, then get stuck in them because they never awoke to the marketplace value of their real talents.

I've had people come to me and say, "I wish I were talented."

I tell them, "You *are* talented." Everyone is talented in something. Don't let anyone convince you otherwise. Your own estimate of your abilities is the most important estimate. So identify your strong points, give them the recognition they deserve, and use them to do what you like to do.

THE SEVEN INTELLIGENCES

Many people become convinced that they are untalented because they can't sing, dance, compose poetry, carve statues, design buildings or write software programs.

But talent can come in many forms. Talent is a form of intelligence, and Harvard scholar Howard Gardner has identified seven basic types of intelligence.[1] They are:

(1) *Logical-mathematical.* This is the intelligence usually measured by IQ tests. It enables people to recognize patterns and order in the world. Logical-thinking people can string together thoughts in logical, coherent patterns. They see clear relationships between cause and effect, and use these relationships to solve problems. Engineers, accountants, physicists, police detectives, and business managers need this form of intelligence.

(2) *Linguistic.* Linguistic intelligence involves more than knowing a lot of words. It also involves the skillful use of words to inspire, influence and instruct. A person with high logical-mathematical intelligence may know a lot of big words and be able to understand complicated writing. But it takes linguistic intelligence to make the language soar and sing. Winston Churchill used his considerable logical/ mathematical intelligence to plot strategies for World War II. He used his extraordinary linguistic intelligence to rally the British people to the Axis challenge. Linguistic intelligence can be invaluable in the fields of writing, broadcasting, public relations, coun-seling, politics, corporate leadership and any other

field requiring the use of words to influence people.

(3) *Spatial.* Spatial intelligence refers to the ability to visualize material objects, manipulate them in the brain, and reproduce them in tangible form. The artist, the sculptor, the architect, the carpenter, the plumber and the garment-maker all employ spatial intelligence.

(4) *Bodily/Kinesthetic.* Have you ever known people who were brilliant thinkers or eloquent communicators but couldn't tie their shoes? Such people may be strong in logical and linguistic intelligence, but lacking in bodily/ kinesthetic intelligence. This is the form of intelligence that lets mind and muscles work together harmoniously. The athlete, the dancer, the juggler and the surgeon need bodily/kinesthetic intelligence.

(5) *Interpersonal.* The person with high interpersonal intelligence has a highly developed ability to "read" other peo-ple. Teachers, psychologists, lawyers, detectives, and salespeople find this type of intelligence valuable in their professions. Interpersonal intelligence is an asset in any undertaking that requires interaction with other people.

(6) *Intrapersonal.* Intrapersonal intelligence is self-understanding. It enables you to look

deep within yourself and make sense of what you see. The gift of introspection can serve you in any pursuit, and can be invaluable in helping you to understand and deal with others. "Know thyself," the inscription on the Delphic Oracle that comes to us through the Greco-Roman writer Plutarch, is an important piece of advice. Shakespeare adds to it some timeless counsel, which I paraphrase this way: Above all, be true to yourself, and as surely as day follows night, you can't be false to anyone.

(7) *Musical.* People with high levels of musical intelligence are sensitive to pitch, melody, rhythm and tone. The ability to make music is an invaluable social asset, and can also lead to a rewarding career. An appreciation for good music can enrich your life immeasurably.

Now stop and think about your own abilities and interests. In which of these intelligences are you the strongest?

YOU DON'T NEED TO BE BRILLIANT

Remember that you don't have to be brilliant to be successful. As Thomas Edison observed, "Genius is one percent inspiration and 99% perspiration." People with seemingly ordinary gifts have made extraordinary contributions to society. The secret lies in determining where your strengths lie, then *focusing* those strengths on your objectives.

Focusing is simply a way of mobilizing and concentrating power. The water in a steam boiler has no more potential than the water in your bathtub. But the water in the steam boiler, when energized and focused, will propel locomotives and drive the wheels of industry. The unfocused, non-energized water in the bathtub just goes down the drain. The talents you possess can remain unfocused and non-energized, in which case all your potential may go down the drain. Or they may be focused and energized, in which case you may become another Harry Truman or Dwight Eisenhower; an Eleanor Roosevelt or Margaret Mitchell.

As Thomas Wolfe, the great North Carolina novelist, wrote:

> *If a man has a talent and cannot use it, he has failed. If he has a talent and uses only half of it, he has partly failed. If he has a talent and learns somehow to use the whole of it, he has gloriously succeeded, and won a satisfaction and a triumph few men ever know.*

So identify your talent and decide to use it in exciting, rewarding ways.

My Strongest Talents

Figure 1-1

On the form above, list as many of your talents as you can think of. To help you identify them, review the seven basic intelligences and look for the ones in which you excel.

Chapter Two

What Do You Enjoy Doing?

*The return from your work must be the sat-
isfaction which that work brings you and the
world's need of that work. With this, life is
heaven, or as near heaven as you can get.
Without this — with work which you
despise, which bores you, and which the
world does not need — this life is hell.*

— William Edward Burghardt du Boiss

Your opportunities for success will be brighter
if you pursue a career that makes the best use of your
talents *and provides you with personal satisfaction.*

That's where the second question comes into
play: *What do you enjoy doing?*

Answering that question will help you identify:

♦ Your *congenial competencies.*
♦ Your *compatible careers.*
♦ Your *congenial roles.*

Let me explain what I mean.

A *congenial competency* is an activity that allows you to use your best talents in an enjoyable and satisfying way.

A *compatible career* is a line of work that allows you to use your congenial competencies in a profitable way.

A *congenial role* is a position within a compatible career that lets you follow your normal behavior pattern most of the time.

To illustrate: You may have a talent for drawing things, and you enjoy making sketches and filling in the details. This is a *congenial competency.*

Your talents can be profitably applied in fields such as architecture, commercial graphics, and cartooning. These are *compatible careers.*

You enjoy interacting with people and being a part of the commercial process, so you decide to become a commercial artist. This is a *congenial role.*

IDENTIFYING YOUR CONGENIAL COMPETENCIES

At the end of Chapter One, you listed your strongest talents, based on the seven basic intelligences. Now think about the ways you enjoy applying those talents. Use Figure 2-2 at the end of this chapter to list them.

To determine what activities give you the most satisfaction, ask yourself these questions:

(1) What do I do that gives me the greatest sense of accomplishment?

(2) What do I do that gives me the greatest feeling of pride?

(3) What do I do that gives me the greatest feeling of confidence?

(4) If I had a year to spend doing anything I wanted, what would I do?

Usually the things you enjoy doing are the things you do well. When you have identified the activities that meet these criteria, you will have identified your *congenial competencies.*

IDENTIFYING YOUR COMPATIBLE CAREERS

Each basic intelligence can be the doorway to a variety of compatible careers. To use a couple of famous examples, Mikhail Baryshnikov and Michael Jordan both excel in bodily/kinesthetic intelligence.

Baryshnikov achieved his greatest satisfaction on the ballet stage. Jordan achieved his on the basketball court. Both rode their *congenial competencies* to stardom in *compatible careers*.

Use figure 2-3 to list the careers in which you can apply your congenial competencies. Start with the company you now work for. Think of the career tracks it offers. You may find opportunities in sales, marketing, design, finance, engineering, public relations, research and development, computer technology, human-resource development and other fields within your organization. Your human-resource department can help you develop a list, and management is always alert for people who are looking for ways to apply their talents more effectively.

T. J. Walker is an example of a young man who found a compatible career after joining a small company, and he enriched himself and the company.

Walker's congenial competency was drawing. At the age of 24, he left the family farm in Mississippi, borrowed his brother's old Honda Civic, and headed for Los Angeles.

There he went to work for Carl Jones, an entrepreneur from Watts. Jones had a profitable enterprise printing designs on clothing. One day they heard some friends discussing the possibility of opening stores that specialized in ethnic clothing. Walker and Jones liked the sound of the idea.

They took a trip to New York, where Walker took his sketch pad into the streets of the inner city to see what the young people were wearing. From these sketches, they designed a line of clothing aimed specifically toward the African American community. They called their enterprise Threads 4 Life, and it caught on rapidly, soon growing into a $70 million-a-year business.

In Woburn, Massachusetts, a 22-year-old man took a job as a forklift repairman at a warehouse. But his real love was computer programming. One day he approached management with a program he designed for a computer-controlled warehousing system. Management liked what it saw — in the warehousing system and in the employee. Soon the young man was prospering in a congenial role in a compatible career — as a full-time software designer.

Your company probably offers you opportunities in a variety of careers that would allow you to practice your congenial competencies in stimulating, exciting ways. If the career doesn't excite you, you won't approach it with enthusiasm — and enthusiasm is necessary to success in any endeavor.

Don't overlook the possibility of "inventing" your own career. We are living in an age of innovation. New technology and new economic and social conditions are creating needs that never before existed. Satisfying those needs may call for enterprises that never before existed.

A New Englander named Preston Smith used innovative thinking to follow his congenial competency to success and wealth.

He studied agricultural science in college and drifted into a job at a screen-printing plant, but that wasn't what he really liked.

What Smith really liked was skiing.

For most people, skiing is a pastime for winter week-ends, but Smith decided that it would make a great *compatible career*. So he decided to open a ski resort on Killington Peak in the Green Mountains of Vermont.

Smith acquired the financial backing, leased some state forest land, then persuaded the state to build a road to his property, based on the potential economic benefits for the area.

Then he added a technological innovation: Until that time, ski resorts had to rely on nature to provide the snow, and nature was notoriously undependable. Smith became the first person to make large-scale use of artificial snow.

Killington Peak became a huge success, and Smith was able to enjoy his favorite activity while making lots of money.

IDENTIFYING YOUR CONGENIAL ROLES

To be completely happy in your work, you have to look beyond your talents and your likes. You also have to consider the type of *behavior* the role will require of you.

It stands to reason that you will be happiest and most successful in roles that allow you to be yourself. This means responding to people, events and circumstances in a way that is most natural and most comfortable for you.

Even when you've found a *congenial competency* in a *compatible career,* you may find roles that require you to behave in ways that make you uncomfortable. For instance, if you enjoy writing, you may thrive in a role that allows you to work in solitude, alone with your creative thoughts. A busy newspaper office, full of jangling telephones, clacking keyboards and loud conversation might be stressful and unpleasant for you. But some writers thrive in the hurly-burly atmosphere of a newsroom and get writer's block when they're alone with their thoughts.

If your *congenial competency* is business management, you may be in your element when you're plotting sales and marketing strategy, but you may be uncomfortable when you have to discipline subordinates, and miserable when you have to fire them. Others may find it stimulating to deal with human-relations problems and may take hiring and firing decisions in stride as part of the normal routine of management.

Therefore, in choosing your roles in life, it's helpful to look at the normal way you respond to people and events.

We generally divide people into four broad behavioral categories. I call them:

Top-Gun
Engaging
Accommodating
Meticulous.

It's no accident that these descriptions form the acronym TEAM, because a good organization should be a team consisting of people from each category. Each behavioral mode can make positive contributions toward organizational success. Individuals, too, need to call on each behavioral mode at appropriate times. Fortunately, each of us is capable of functioning in any of the modes, though we usually have one that we prefer most of the time. That's the one I refer to as your *preferred behavioral mode*.

Here is a brief description of each mode:

TOP-GUN

People who prefer the *top-gun* mode are extroverted, action-oriented and motivated to win. They are more comfortable when giving orders than they are when receiving them.

Their greatest fear is losing. For them, it is a painful experience, and they will go to great lengths to avoid it, often ignoring the feelings of those who stand between them and their objectives.

In conversation, *top-guns* like to skip the preliminaries and cut to the chase. They are impatient with details. They prefer to plot grand strategy and let others worry about tactics.

Top-guns work best in jobs that allow them considerable latitude for decision-making. They want their bosses to give them their assignments, then stand aside while they get the job done — *their* way.

ENGAGING

Engaging people are also extroverted and action-oriented, but they are more relaxed and playful than *top-gun* people are. Winning is important to them, but being liked and admired is even more important.

Engaging people are often social leaders, and on the job they excel at tasks that involve working with other people. Their bright, enthusiastic personalities usually promote high morale and encourage teamwork. They are usually miserable when forced to work alone. They relish friendly competition, and will exert themselves to be the best at what they do.

Engagers like to warm up with small talk before getting down to the business at hand. Whereas *top-guns* might frown on chit-chat around the water cooler as a waste of time, *engaging* people see it as an opportunity to forge relationships. *Engaging* people use their socializing skills to create networks of people they can call upon when needed.

Engagers usually are self-confident, and sometimes they overestimate their competence. They may accept challenges before they have acquired the skills to meet them, and may implement new ideas before they have been adequately tested.

Their greatest fear is public embarrassment. A visible mistake committed in the presence of others, or criticism delivered in front of work mates can be devastating to their morale.

Engaging people, like *top-guns*, are more interested in the big picture than they are in the details. They are good at organizing group efforts, setting the overall objective and assigning the details to others.

They often are unaware of time, and tend to let deadlines sneak up on them. But they are also good at getting things done at the last minute.

ACCOMMODATING

Accommodating persons are friendly introverts. Being an introvert doesn't mean that you dislike the company of others. It means that when your emotional batteries are running low, you prefer to recharge them by seeking some quiet time to yourself where you can relax and meditate. Extroverts recharge their emotional batteries by interacting with others.

Accommodating persons are motivated by a desire to be liked. This need to be liked may lead them to subordinate their own interests to the interests of others.

Accommodators are diplomatic. They work smoothly with people who follow all three of the other behavioral modes. They make good teachers and counselors because they are highly empathetic. They can "feel" what other people are feeling. But they also have to guard against shouldering the burdens that others should carry for themselves.

Accommodators are loyal, dependable people who can work either alone or in cooperation with others. They like peaceful, predictable environments.

Because they dislike conflict, *accommodating* people will avoid directly challenging others. They will challenge or criticize indirectly, often using hints or coded messages. They are quite sensitive to nuances in speech and manners, and assume that others are similarly attuned. The *top-gun's* no-nonsense straight talk turns them off.

Accommodators like to find comfortable routines and follow them. They prize security, and are uncomfortable with change.

Accommodating people don't like to advertise their virtues. They prefer to let their actions speak for themselves. Yet they expect their work to be recognized and appreciated. If it isn't, they feel hurt.

Accommodators are good planners, and although they tend to be non-aggressive, their ability to act should not be underestimated. Dwight Eisenhower preferred the *accommodating* behavioral mode, and he led the planning for the greatest military invasion in history. When it came time to fish or cut bait at Normandy, Eisenhower weighed the risks and acted. The Nazi generals learned that they weren't confronted by a doormat.

METICULOUS

Meticulous people, like *accommodating* people, are introverted. They are highly logical, detail-oriented people. Unlike *engaging* people, they don't need the company of other people. They can work alone for hours, energized by the challenge of applying logic to a knotty problem. Unlike *accommodating* people, they don't need to be liked for their personal qualities. They are content to be judged by the quality of their work. Unlike *top-guns*, their principal motivation is not winning. They often seem indifferent to applause, and to them being correct is more important than being liked.

When Henry Clay, the 19th century American statesman, said "I'd rather be right than be president," he was voicing sentiments that *meticulous* people can readily identify with. Their chief motivation is the achievement of the high standards they set for themselves.

Meticulous people aim for quality and consistency. They are analytical, disciplined, thorough and precise. They are cautious, and will not take action until they are sure the circumstances are right.

Don't get into arguments with *meticulous* persons unless you're sure of your ground. They know the manuals and rule books. They are comfortable with statistics, and absorb information like sponges.

Like *top-guns*, meticulous people dislike small talk. They just want the facts. They see criticism of their work as personal criticism, but they appreciate a constructive approach. Show them or tell them how to do things better, and you'll get a positive response.

WHICH IS YOUR PREFERRED MODE?

Which of these behavioral modes best fits the way you respond most of the time?

Possibly you can discern in yourself some of the qualities of each mode. That's because, at one time or another, we step into each of the modes.

You can get a general idea of the mode you prefer by answering these questions:

(1) When you want someone to do something for you, do you communicate by giving an order or by making a suggestion?

(2) When you're working on a project with other people, which gets most of your attention: the job you have to do or the people you're working with?

	Directing	Suggesting	Relationship	Task
Meticulous				
Accommodating				
Engaging				
Top-Gun				

Figure 2-1

Figure 2-1 shows how your responses relate to your preferred mode. *Top-gun* people normally communicate by telling people directly what to do. They focus more on the tasks than on their relationships with the people performing the tasks. *Engaging* people normally communicate their desires directly too, but they focus their attention on relationships instead of tasks. *Accommodating* people are more comfortable making suggestions than giving orders. Their focus is on relationships. *Meticulous* people also communicate by suggestion rather than by direct order. They focus on tasks over relationships.

To pinpoint your behavioral pattern more definitively, I recommend the use of such instruments as the Performax™ personal profiles and the Myers-Briggs Type Indicator. A version of the Myers-Briggs Type Indicator may be found in the book **_Please Understand Me_**, by David Keirsey and Marilyn Bates (Del Mar, California: Prometheus Nemesis Book Company, 1984). The book **_People Smart_** (La Jolla, California: Keynote Publishing Company, 1990) by Tony Allesandra and Michael J. O'Connor, is devoted to a discussion of Performax™ behavioral styles.

IDENTIFYING CONGENIAL ROLES

Knowing your preferred behavioral mode can help you identify your *congenial roles* in the career of your choice.

Suppose you enjoy sports and have a high bodily/kinesthetic intelligence. You also enjoy working with young people. Based on these factors, you think you might enjoy a career as an athletic coach.

Your preferred behavioral mode is *accommodating*. This means that you value security, dislike personal conflict, and prefer to influence others through suggestion rather than direct instructions.

Think about how these preferences would affect your performance as a coach.

A Coach's job security often depends upon the ability to turn out winning teams year after year. But your principal motivation is not winning, but being liked. Can you stretch beyond your preferred mode and take on the *top-gun*'s winning instincts when necessary? Can you live with the insecurity of knowing that one mediocre season could send you back into the job market? Will you be able to tell an athlete who has worked her heart out for a position on the squad that she didn't make the cut? Will you be able to discipline the *top gun* player who thinks he knows better than you how to run the team?

These are situations you may face that will require you to step outside your preferred mode.

That doesn't mean that an accommodating person should forget about being a coach. Many excellent athletic coaches and managers follow the accommodating behavioral mode most of the time. Moreover, people sometimes follow different preferred modes under different circumstances. Casey Stengel, the great baseball manager, could be a talkative, sometimes clownish *engager* when dealing with the press and the public, then turn into a no-nonsense *top-gun* when dealing with his players.

As you consider your role in life, keep in mind your preferred mode and the extent to which you will have to stretch beyond it to achieve success. Decide whether you can make the stretch without encountering an unacceptable level of stress. Then make your choice.

GOOD GENERALS, DIFFERENT MODES

To see how different behavioral modes can affect individuals who pursue careers in harmony with their congenial competencies, let's examine the cases of three American Generals who gained fame during World War II: George Patton, Dwight Eisenhower, and Douglas MacArthur.

Patton was an extremely gifted military tactician. He loved the calling. A military career was thoroughly compatible with the values he held. An assertive, dominating leader, he loved victory and hated defeat. He exemplified the *top-gun* behavioral mode. The military was clearly his natural calling.

But not all military roles were compatible with his preferred behavioral mode.

On the battlefield, he could give his *top-gun* mode full rein. He was doing what he did best, and his aggressive, win-at-all-costs style contributed to his success.

But Patton never was placed in charge of an entire theater and never made it to the highest levels of military rank. The top jobs went to men like

Eisenhower, George C. Marshall, and Omar N. Bradley — men who could deal with the sensitive egos of world-class statesmen and of other military commanders without stepping outside their behavioral modes.

Eisenhower's *accommodating* mode served him well when he was plotting strategy with Winston Churchill, Franklin Roosevelt and the top Allied military brains. But he knew when to step outside his preferred mode. Fortunately, he was able to do so on the eve of D-Day. The success of the Normandy landings depended upon favorable weather. The weather had been bad for some time, and the forecasters were not sure it would clear up in time for the landings. Eisenhower had to decide whether to delay the invasion, and thus give the enemy more time to discover Allied plans and fortify strategic points, or to give the go-ahead and risk disaster on the beaches. If the landings failed, the liberation of Europe would be delayed — perhaps forever.

Every instinct of the *accommodating* behavioral mode must have urged Ike to take the cautious approach.

But the general weighed the risks and decided to go ahead. Before retiring for the night, he wrote a note, to be released in event the landings failed. In it, he took full responsibility for the failure. Ike had stepped into the *top-gun* mode to make his decision. He stepped back into the *accommodating* mode to take the blame for the possible failure.

General MacArthur was another superb commander who could follow his preferred behavioral mode to victory against the Japanese in the Pacific. But when he was put in command of United Nations forces in Korea, he was in a role that conflicted with his behavioral mode. World War II called for an all-out victory effort. In Korea, the military objectives were often subordinated to political objectives, which went against MacArthur's values and instincts. Unwilling to step outside his behavioral mode to accommodate the political realities, he eventually was relieved of command.

Both Patton and MacArthur had talent in spades, but when they had to step outside their preferred behavioral modes, they were unable to apply their talents with full effect.

GO FOR THE POSITIVE

Each role you contemplate will match up with your preferred behavioral mode in a positive, a negative or a neutral way.

If the role you want to fill is a negative match with your preferred behavioral mode, it means that you will have to exert extra effort to succeed. You will be tacking into the wind and swimming against the current. Success will come harder.

If your role is a neutral match, you will be navigating in calm winds and still water. Resistance may be light, but you'll have to provide the momentum.

If you have a positive match, then you will be sailing with the current and have the wind at your back. Success will be much easier to achieve. You will be in a congenial role.

Look for the career that will be the best fit for your talents and the role that will be the best fit for your disposition. A congenial role within a compatible career offers you the surest route to success.

Determine Your Congenial Competencies

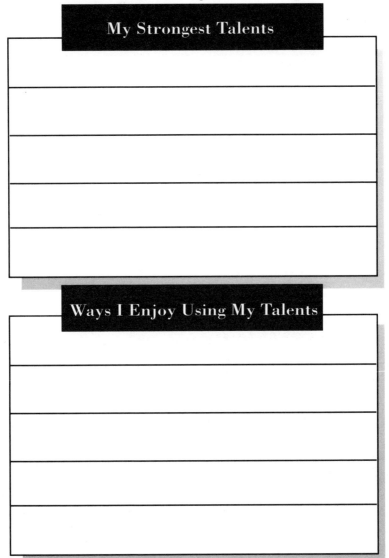

My Strongest Talents

Ways I Enjoy Using My Talents

Figure 2-2

The exercises on these pages are designed to help you identify the careers that offer you the best opportunities to use your talents, and the roles within those careers that are most compatible with your talents and your behavioral mode.

In Figure 2-2, above, list your strongest talents in column 1. In cloumn 2, list the things you enjoy doing that utilize these talents. These are your congenial competencies. List them in column 1 of Figure 2-3 on the next page.

41

Determine Your Compatible Careers

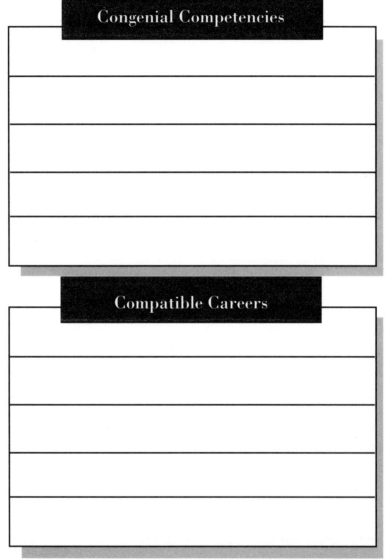

Congenial Competencies

Compatible Careers

Figure 2-3

In column 1 of Figure 2-3, above, list the congenial competencies from column 2 of figure 2-2. Now think of the careers in which you can use your congenial competencies, starting with the career tracks in your present organization. List them in column 2, under Compatible Careers.

Determine Your Congenial Roles

Compatible Careers

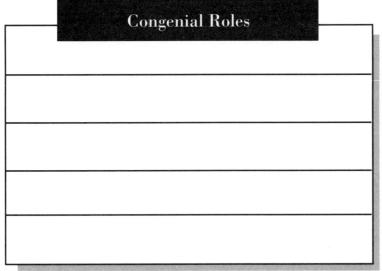

Congenial Roles

Figure 2-4

In column 1, list the compatible careers you identified in Figure 2-3. In column 2, list the roles in which you would feel most comfortable. If your compatible career is business, for instance, your congenial role might be as a manager, an account executive or a financial officer.

43

Chapter Three

What Values Are Important To You?

We may be personally defeated, but our principles never.

— **William Lloyd Garrison**

You've learned so far how to identify your *congenial competencies*, your *compatible careers* and your *congenial roles*. In other words, your career choices can now be guided by:

♦ The things you like to do.

♦ The things you do best.

♦ Your preferred behavioral mode.

But true success goes far beyond a career choice. The history books and entertainment magazines are full of examples of people whose careers soared while their lives crashed — even as they were doing the things they enjoyed and did best.

This can happen if your behavior is not in line with *rules of conduct* based on a *set of principles* grounded in *positive personal values*.

Don't worry. I'm not going to give you a set of rules to tell you what you can and can't do with your life. But you can write your own rules, based on the principles you choose and the values you cherish.

Let's stop to define what we mean.

A *value* is something you hold dear.

A *principle* is a broad, fundamental truth.

A *rule of conduct* is a guide to behavior designed to implement a principle.

Examples:

Human life is a *value*.

"It is wrong to take human life deliberately and maliciously" is a *principle*.

"Thou shalt not commit murder" is a *rule of conduct*.

The principle supports the value; the rule implements the principle.

Different people value different things. You may view some values as negative and some as positive. Some people value generosity, kindness and decency. Others value greed, violence and obscenity.

What you value determines the principles by which you measure your behavior.

Sound principles are based on your rock-bottom assessment of what is right. They represent your perception of the way things ought to be in relation to your values. If you want to be truly happy, direct your efforts toward bringing your life into harmony with the way things ought to be.

All the talent in the world will not bring you happiness if it is not applied in harmony with this perception of the way things should be. Applying your talents without reference to your values and principles is like using your car's accelerator without touching the steering wheel. It may take you far and fast, but it probably won't take you where you want to go. And it may take you over a cliff or into a brick wall.

MERGING THE IMAGES

Most of us see life like a split image viewed through the focusing lens of a camera. One image represents reality: the way things are. The other represents our principles: the way things ought to be. Successful people bring their lives into focus by merging the two images. When we perceive the way things are as the way things ought to be, our lives are in harmony.

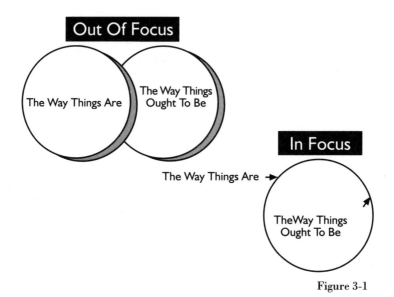

Figure 3-1

WHAT'S IMPORTANT TO YOU?

Merging the two images means much more than finding the right career. It involves the whole spectrum of your life's activities. To become truly successful, you must examine your life in all its aspects and determine what things are important to you; what things are worthy to receive your energy and your attention; what values will motivate you to put forth your maximum efforts.

For many people, a career is the value at the center of their lives. Everything they do revolves around the job. It becomes their *core motivation*.

For others, a career is a means to an end. Its role is to provide them with the financial ability to do the things that are really important to them. Their core motivations lie outside their careers.

Your core motivation springs from the values you deem to be most important in your life. No one can tell you what values you should put first in your life. That's a conclusion that you yourself must reach. It's a conclusion that will guide your most vigorous efforts. We tend to expend the most time and energy on the things we consider important.

CONSCIOUS AND UNCONSCIOUS CHOICES

The choice between what's important and what's unimportant in your life can be made either consciously or unconsciously.

The husband and father who spends most of his time in front of a television, ignoring the activities of his household and neglecting the training of his children may not have decided consciously that the tube is more important than his wife and family, but the choice has been made. And to him, television *is* important.

The woman who spends her bonus on an expensive new sports car instead of investing it in a retirement fund may not have made a conscious decision to value material possessions ahead of financial security, but she has indeed decided that present pleasures are more important to her than future comfort.

People whose reading habits tend toward romance novels, sports magazines and horoscopes to the exclusion of self-help books, professional journals and business publications may not have decided consciously that leisure-time pleasures are more important than their careers, but their activities indicate that the decisions have been made.

A few people have followed unconscious choices to spectacular success — simply because their choices happened to place them in the right places at the right times. Others have meandered through life pursuing whatever passion occupied the place of importance at the moment and ended up going nowhere. Unconscious choices put you at the mercy of the dice roll.

TWICE A STABLE HAND

I once heard a story about an old peasant in medieval times who served as a stable hand on the nobleman's estate. One day a wizard happened by and watched him laboring away.

"Is a stable hand all you were meant to be?" the wizard asked.

"I don't rightly know," said the old man.

"I have the power to turn you into whatever you'd like to become," said the wizard. "Make up your mind, and when I come back by in a couple of weeks I'll grant your wish."

The stable man decided that the easiest way to decide what he would like to be was to wander around the estate, observing people and noting the ones he felt most drawn toward.

He felt no great attraction toward the miller or the cobbler or even toward the nobleman and his family. The miller's job was too strenuous; he didn't like the idea of lifting all those bags of grain and flour. The cobbler's job required too many skills; he didn't want to expend the time and effort to acquire them. And he didn't care for the weighty responsibilities that burdened the nobleman.

Finally, he happened across a peasant woman rocking her baby in front of her cottage. He felt a strong attachment for the baby.

So when the wizard returned in two weeks, the old man told him, "I want to be a baby."

The wizard granted his wish. Fifty years later — he being gifted with immortality — the wizard happened past the same barn.

And there he saw the same old peasant cleaning out the stable.

Instead of proactively deciding what he wanted to become, the stable man left it to passive choice. And what he got was predictable.

DON'T DRIFT INTO A CHOICE

You don't have to drift into a choice of core motivation. You can decide consciously what values you *choose* to make the center of your life. You can arrange your values in order of priority and allocate your time and energy on the basis of these choices.

Remember that your core value is what you place at the center of your life. It will govern the direction in which you expend your most vigorous efforts.

Your core value may be people, possessions, activities or principles. It may be strong or weak and it may be conscious or unconscious, but everybody has one.

THE PERSON-CENTERED LIFE

Those who put people at the center of their lives are governed by the needs of the other person.

We've all known parents who focused their entire lives around doing things for their children or grandchildren. We've known wives and husbands who devoted their principal energies to making their spouses happy. We've known people who expended their lives promoting the interests of a politician or a religious figure. We've even known people who spent all their resources following an entertainment or sports idol on their tours.

When you empower another person in this way, you disempower yourself. You are taking away from yourself the power of independent decision-making and placing all your decisions, directly or indirectly, in the hands of the other person.

In extreme cases, we see the spouses or off-spring of people with substance-abuse or other emotional problems centering their lives on the person with the problem. They try to compensate for the other person's behavior by modifying their own. They weigh each aspect of their conduct in the light of its possible effect on the behavior of the dysfunctional person. Such behavior has a label: co-dependency. It not only is ineffective in helping the person with the problem; it also destroys the lives of the co-dependents.

You can also put people at the core of your motivation by making them the objects of your hatred. The movie *Amadeus* portrayed the destructiveness of this type of obsession in the case of the envious musician who devoted his life to sabotaging the career of Mozart.

THE LIFE CENTERED ON POSSESSIONS

People who put material possessions at the center of their lives concentrate on *acquiring* things rather than *using* things. They're like the king who keeps his gold in a vault and derives his pleasure from visiting his treasure.

Stew Leonard, my friend who has gained fame through his innovative management practices at his Connecticut dairy store, likes to tell the story of such a king.

Once a peasant offered to pay the king an extra farthing in taxes if the king would let him see the room where the gold was kept.

The king, ever alert for a chance to augment his fortune, let the peasant have a look.

The peasant peered at the heap of shiny yellow metal and remarked, "Now I'm as rich as you are."

The king was puzzled.

"This room holds more than half the gold in the kingdom," he said, "and it all belongs to me. How can you be as rich as I?"

The peasant replied: "You have all this gold and all you do is look at it. Now I too have looked at it."

WHEN ACTIVITIES ARE AT THE CENTER

People who put activities at the core of their motivation may become involved in an endless rat race that leads to few lasting rewards. Activities might include such things as a career, sports, music, entertainment, hobbies, church and travel.

All of these things are worthy objects of your efforts. But if you settle upon any of them as your *core motivation*, you greatly narrow the scope of your efforts and greatly restrict your prospects for happiness. People who put career first may end up with gold-plated resumes and rusted-out family lives. People who put sports, music and entertainment first may go through life having a ball but going home in tears after the ball is over. Happiness isn't the same thing as having a ball.

People who pursue church activities to the exclusion of family and personal obligations may find that their families resent being short-changed and that their excessive zeal is giving the church a bad name. Jesus himself spoke against those who allowed the forms and rituals of religion to crowd out the overall principle of love, and the apostle Paul warned of those with "a form of Godliness but having denied the power thereof."[1]

CENTERING YOUR LIFE ON PRINCIPLES

The most stable and enduring source of core motivation is a positive, well-thought-out set of principles by which you choose to live your life. Your principles are based on your values: the most important things in your life.

When your life is people-centered, the important thing to you is what others want.

When your life is possession-centered, the important thing is what you have.

When it is activity-centered, the important thing is what you do.

When it is principle-centered, the important thing is who and what you are.

The principles we live by determine our character — the essence of who we are. When we live by our principles we are being true to ourselves.

Your principles, can be like a compass, quickly pointing in the right direction when crisis time arrives. They can be like an anchor, providing a source of steadiness amid tumultuous circumstances. And they can be like the nozzle of a hose — directing the stream of your thoughts and efforts in a purposeful way while concentrating their power on the things that matter.

A YOUTHFUL LAMENT

In this age of frenetic change, people without a firm set of principles may find themselves in the position of the young people described by a staff writer for the Detroit Free Press:

> We're in our 20s. We should be having fun, like all those people in all those Pepsi commercials. Instead, so many of us are in crisis.

> It began with a few uncomfortable moments. We started using moisturizer every night or cooking sit-down meals or opening Individual Retirement Accounts. Or we started thinking we **should**.

> It grew until it became more troubling than maintaining a wrinkle-free existence or using the food in the refrigerator

before it went bad. It grew until we began re-evaluating the very essence of our lives.

*The questions: "Am I happy? Am I successful? Is my relationship all wrong? Do I even have a relationship? Why **don't** I have a relationship? Is the world going to become an even scarier place?*

Who am I, anyway?

The answers: I don't know. I don't know. I don't know" . . .

This uncomfortable, restless feeling is keeping many of us awake at night. And hanging with us all day, weighing on every decision, every movement of our lives.[2]

BE QUICK TO DECIDE, SLOW TO CHANGE

Successful people don't lie awake nights agonizing over decisions and directions. They're quick to decide and slow to change their minds. Unsuccessful people are often slow to decide and quick to change their minds.

The difference lies in the fact that successful people are guided by a set of constant principles. They take decisions that are in harmony with these principles. Their decisions therefore are as solid as their principles. They don't second-guess themselves and seldom reverse themselves.

Laws and rules may be flexible, for they must take into account a variety of circumstances. Hence, criminal laws specify different degrees of punishment for different levels of homicide.

But, in the words of Abraham Lincoln, "Important principles may and must be inflexible." If principles can be bent, they cannot serve as reliable guides to behavior.

You can choose the principles you want to guide you by first deciding on the values you hold dear.

IDENTIFYING YOUR GUIDING PRINCIPLES

Figures 3-2 through 3-4 will help you identify the values and principles you want to live by.

First, think of the roles that are important to you in your family, vocational life, community life and religious life. Now think of the people, activities, and qualities you value in each role.

For each value, write a supporting principle. Make it personal. State it in the form of a sentence describing yourself as you would like to be, in the light of these values. Do this for each of the roles that are important to you.

For example, if one of your values is *honesty*, you might write as your supporting principles in your role as a business person:

1. *I can be relied on at all times to tell the truth.*

2. *I never take more than I am entitled to or pay less than my fair obligation.*

3. *I do not engage in deceptive practices.*

If one of your values is *financial prosperity,* you might write as your supporting principles:

1. *I never miss an opportunity to upgrade my career qualifications.*

2. *I take intelligent risks in investing my time and resources.*

3. *I look for ways to enhance the perceived value of my products or services in the eyes of potential customers or clients.*

HOW CAN YOU APPLY THEM?

When you have identified the principles you want to guide your life, use them in measuring each possible career and role choice. When you have found a pursuit that conforms to your basic principles while allowing you to do what you do best and enjoy most in your preferred behavior mode, you will have found your ideal calling.

Go for it.

EXERCISES

In Figures 3-2 through 3-5 on the following pages, use the left column of each form to list the values that are important to you in each major area of your life. Use the right column to list the personal behavioral principles that support each of these values. Use the values and principles as guides for decision-makming in each area of life.

Values and Principles in My Family Life

Values	Supporting Principles

Figure 3-2

Values and Principles in My Career

Values	Supporting Principles

Figure 3-3

Values and Principles in My Spiritual Life

Values	Supporting Principles

Figure 3-4

Values and Principles in My Civic Life

Values	Supporting Principles

Figure 3-5

64

Chapter Four

The Art of the Possible

God, give us the grace to accept with sereni-ty the things that cannot be changed, courage to change the things which should be changed, and the wisdom to distinguish the one from the other.

— Reinhold Niebuhr

Once you have decided what things to place at the center of your life, your next step is to focus on the areas that you can effectively influence.

Some of the things that are important to you may be beyond your area of influence.

Music may be an important part of your life, and you may dream of singing on Broadway. But if you sing like a bullfrog with laryngitis, it's unlikely that you will be able to will your way into a Broadway role.

But that doesn't put music appreciation beyond your area of influence. You can enjoy going to performances, and you can learn the lyrics and sing along in the privacy of your home or automobile. You can also learn to play an instrument.

You may find that the adorable person you married has a chemical-dependence problem, or has a violent temper, or is a poor money manager. You may offer your spouse your support and encouragement in overcoming these problems, but they actually lie outside your area of effective influence. The only person who can overcome an addiction is the addict; the only person who can control a violent temper is the individual with the violent temper; the only one who can change sloppy money-management habits for the better is the individual who has the sloppy habits.

You may face many limitations that you can do nothing about. If you have poor eyesight and poor reflexes, you won't make it on the professional tennis circuit. If you're six-feet-seven and weigh 270 pounds, forget about being a jockey. If your logical/ mathematical intelligence is average but no higher, you probably won't make it as a nuclear physicist, no matter how hard you study. If your bodily/kinesthetic intelligence is such that you have trouble threading a needle and tying a knot, do us all a favor and avoid a career as a brain surgeon.

PICK YOUR BATTLES

Good generals know that the secret to winning wars is to pick your battle sites. Try not to wage a campaign on unfavorable terrain. Avoid head-on confrontations when the enemy has superior numbers and fire power.

That doesn't mean giving up. It means directing your efforts toward the situations you can influence and not wasting your energy on things beyond your control or things that don't really matter.

The Battle of Midway, the turning point in the Pacific during World War II, illustrates the point. American air power at that point was no match for the Japanese, who had numerical superiority and better fighter aircraft. American airmen had repeatedly sacrificed themselves going head to head with superior Japanese forces. But American intelligence cracked the Japanese radio codes and helped U.S. naval forces locate the Japanese fleet attempting to capture the strategic island of Midway. American dive bombers caught the Japanese carriers when their defending aircraft were off in pursuit of an earlier wave of torpedo bombers, and they were able to put their bombs on the carrier decks. Once the Americans sank the carriers, it was unnecessary to engage the fighters in combat. With no place to land, they simply ran out of fuel and splashed down in the Pacific. The American forces found their area of effective influence and exploited it.

On the home front, too, the United States exploited its area of effective influence. American know-how was soon producing aircraft that could match the prowess of the Japanese planes, and U.S. industrial capacity was producing them at a rate neither the Japanese nor their German and Italian allies could match.

Helen Keller found her area of effective influence in a quite different arena. She couldn't change the fact that she was unable to see or hear. So she directed her energies toward developing other methods of communication, and she achieved sterling success.

Thomas Edison learned the telegrapher's trade while working for the Michigan Central Railroad. At first, the signals were transmitted in the form of dots and dashes scratched on a piece of paper. Later, the signals were transmitted in the form of audible clicks. Edison was hearing-impaired and couldn't hear the clicks.

He didn't waste time trying to improve his hearing, and he didn't strain his ears trying to hear the clicks. Instead, he invented a telegraph that could convert the electric impulses into letters of the alphabet.

SITUATIONAL TRIAGE

The situations you encounter in life generally fall into three categories:

(1) Those you want to influence and can.
(2) Those you'd like to influence but can't.
(3) Those that are not worth influencing.

Choosing the areas on which to focus your energies thus becomes an exercise in situational triage. Triage is a system developed during warfare for classifying the wounded. In one group are placed the people who are likely to die regardless of the treatment they receive. In another group are the people who are likely to survive regardless of whether they receive immediate treatment. In a third are those likely to die without treatment but who might be saved through immediate treatment.

Those in the latter category are the ones who get priority at the field hospitals.

Situational Triage: Effort Where It Counts

You can maximize your chances of success by applying the principles of triage to your challenges. Ignore the challenges that are unlikely to affect your success and happiness either way. Look for ways to adjust to those situations that you can do nothing about. Focus your efforts on the things you can change.

Suppose you're offered an attractive job in a *compatible career*. You're told: "The job requires a familiarity with Lotus software, and you'll need to work an occasional week-end. By the way, you'll be based in Seattle."

You've never worked with Lotus software. You'd prefer to have your Saturdays and Sundays free. And your spouse has a good-paying and secure job in Atlanta.

You think it over and perform situational triage:

You've learned other software programs and you're certain you can master Lotus in a short time. This is a situation well within your area of effective influence.

You like to have Saturdays and Sundays off, but an occasional working week-end wouldn't seriously disrupt your life. This is a situation not worth making an issue over.

The job, though, is in Seattle. You can't change that circumstance, so you must adjust to the reality. You can adjust in a number of ways. You might:

(1) Turn down the job and look for a comparable position in the Atlanta area.

(2) Try to persuade your spouse to pull up stakes and move with you to Seattle.

(3) Agree to a transcontinental marriage, with you on the West Coast and your spouse in the Southeast, spending occasional week-ends together.

(4) Divorce your spouse and start a new life in Seattle.

Note that while the *situation itself* is beyond your control, your *response* to it definitely lies within your area of effective action.

CONSULT YOUR VALUES AND PRINCIPLES

Your decision would have to be made after consulting your values and principles. If family togetherness and love of spouse are among your core values, and you are committed to the principle of marital stability, then the third and fourth options would be unthinkable. You could dismiss them decisively without a second thought. The second option would be viable only if your spouse were willing to make the sacrifice; so it would not lie entirely within your area of effective influence. You probably would exercise the first option. But the choice would be yours.

Many people allow the things they can't control to govern their decision-making. That's the *reactive* approach. Others look for ways to get maximum leverage from the things they *can* control. That's the *proactive* approach.

For instance, even if you decided to turn down the job in Seattle, you could still upgrade your skills so that when a comparable position arose in the Atlanta area you would be ready to claim it. You could compile a list of similar businesses in Atlanta and inquire about their needs in your field of expertise. You might even expand your job search to Birmingham and Chattanooga, assuming your spouse would be willing to live somewhere in between and accept a long commute for the sake of your career.

DON'T SURRENDER TO CIRCUMSTANCES

Accepting the things you can't change doesn't mean that you surrender to circumstances. Proactive people look for ways to succeed *in spite of* the circumstances.

Reactive people are likely to go through life complaining about their circumstances. They focus on things they can do nothing about and ignore the things that are within their circle of influence.

If you live in a northern state, you can stay inside during the winter and complain about the snow and the cold. Or you can take up snow sledding and skiing.

If you live in a large city, you can complain about traffic congestion and the cost of parking, or you can car pool or use public transportation.

If you're a high-school graduate, you can complain about the scarcity of jobs for people without college or technical training, or you can go out and get an education.

If you live in a sparsely settled area that offers limited opportunities in your area of expertise, you can lament the lack of opportunity there or you can take effective action. The action could mean moving to a more populous area that offers the economic opportunities you seek, or it could involve finding ways to use your talents profitably in a sparsely populated area.

If you're an apartment dweller and dream of a home in the suburbs, you can complain about the high cost of real estate, or you can open a savings account and save toward a down payment.

DON'T MISTAKE THE DIFFICULT FOR THE IMPOSSIBLE

A word of caution: Don't be too quick to assign a situation to the second category in your situational triage. Conventional wisdom holds that if you're shorter than the average man you should forget about a professional basketball career, but Muggsy Bogues, who stands 5-feet-three, not only made the team but also became a star with the National Basketball Association's Charlotte Hornets.

It's easy to mistake the difficult for the impossible. And sometimes, things that appear to be impossible are easy enough, if you take the proactive approach.

The situations that lie outside your area of effective influence generally fall into one or the other of these categories:

♦ *Situations resulting from the behavior of others.*

You can't change other people; they have to change themselves. The only situations you can change are those relating to your own behavior.

73

If your business partner has a drinking problem and tends to become obnoxious and alienate clients and customers, you can't force the partner to stop drinking, or to stop seeing clients and customers. But that doesn't mean you have to put up with the consequences of your partner's behavior.

You *can* try to arrange business encounters in non-alcoholic settings. You *can* establish your own personal relationships with clients and customers. And you *can* give your partner an ultimatum: Discontinue the objectionable behavior and get help for the problem or discontinue the partnership. Just be sure that you're able and willing to stand behind the ultimatum. When you take these steps, you're directing your own behavior in a proactive way, and you're not assuming responsibility for your partner's behavior.

> ♦ *Situations resulting from circumstances over which you have no control.*

Things that happened in the past are beyond your control. Forget about them and focus your efforts on the future. If you introduced a product or service that bombed, you can't go back and de-introduce it. Start thinking about what you can do in the future to make up for the failure. If you followed a hot tip on the stock market and got badly burned, you can't breathe life back into the worthless stock. Learn from the experience and move forward.

Accidents of birth are beyond your control. If you were born into a poor family without the means to send you to Harvard Business School or to MIT, you can't go back and trade your parents in on a set of millionaires. If you were born with a physical disability, you can't trade your body in on a better model.

But remember that the cards you're dealt are less important than the way you play your hand. Circumstances may be beyond your control, but you have full control of your responses to circumstances. The history books are full of success stories about people who focused their energies on the things they *could* do rather than the things they couldn't do.

Abraham Lincoln was reared in poverty in the backwoods environments of Kentucky and Southern Illinois. He received very little formal education. Harvard or MIT? He didn't even get through grade school. Yet he became a successful lawyer and perhaps our most eloquent president.

Winston Churchill, while heading Britain's admiralty during World War I, suffered severe criticism after British forces were defeated in their efforts to open up the straits at the Dardanelles and take the Turkish port of Gallipoli. But he didn't let that circumstance of the past dampen confidence in his ability to lead the British to victory in World War II.

Franklin Roosevelt was stricken with polio and couldn't stand without braces; yet he was the 20th century's most powerful president.

Stephen Hawking was stricken with a debilitating disease that left him practically a prisoner in his own body. Yet he became one of the century's outstanding scientists, giving the scientific community dazzling insights into the nature of black holes.

WITHOUT A LEG TO STAND ON

There are some less visible but hardly less dramatic examples of people who achieved success by focusing on the possible. I came across two such examples while browsing through a single issue of *Reader's Digest*.

At West Point, Frederick Franks was captain of the baseball team and planned to follow his *congenial competency* into a successful military career.

His career took him to Indo China. There, Major Franks encountered an exploding grenade in Cambodia. Flying shrapnel shredded his leg, and he had to have it amputated.

Franks couldn't alter the fact that he was an amputee. That circumstance had to go into the second category of triage: something beyond his ability to influence.

But he refused to place his military career and his love for baseball in the same category. He stayed in the Army. He also continued to play baseball. He would go to bat, hit the ball and let a teammate run for him.

Then one day he saw a teammate slide into third, and he thought: "What's the worst that could happen if I tried the same thing?"

On his next trip to the plate, he hit the ball into deep center field. This time, he decided to do his own running. He ran to first as fast as his one good leg and his artificial limb would carry him. He rounded first and jogged toward second. He saw the outfielder throw the ball toward second. Franks slid head-first into the bag and heard the umpire call "Safe!" He was on with a double!

He was just as determined in his military career. Once he led his squadron through field exercises over rough and swampy terrain. When his prosthesis became stuck in the mud, he would tell his men, "That's what happens when you don't have a leg to stand on."

Frederick Franks rose to the rank of four-star general, and became living proof of the effectiveness of focusing on the possible.

"Losing a leg has taught me that a limitation is as big or small as you make it," he said. "The key is to concentrate on what you have, not what you don't have."[1]

A YOUNG GOLFER GETS A HAND

Larry Alford was a young high-school student in a suburb of Houston. He had high bodily/ kinesthetic intelligence and a love of golf. He won a spot in a golf tournament for the country's top young golfers at Rancho, Mirage, California, and he tied for second place. Larry wanted to be a golf pro, and for him that calling represented a *congenial role* in a *compatible career*. He won an athletic scholarship to the University of Houston, and his dreams seemed to be on their way to fulfillment.

Then he was involved in an automobile accident and lost a hand.

Many people would have placed golfing in category two of their situational triage: a circumstance beyond their control. The PGA doesn't have a category for one-handed golfers.

But Larry Alford kept golfing within his area of effective influence. He was placed in a rehabilitation institute, and while there he practiced his putts on the floor of his hospital room. Then he went out to the lawn behind the rehab center and tried a one-handed swing. The ball went 50 yards.

"I'm on the comeback trail," Larry said.

Then Jay Hall, a psychologist who was dating Larry's divorced mother, gave him a hand — literally.

Hall decided to design a prosthetic hand for Larry. If the hand was to control a golf club during the swing, it had to be able to grip the club firmly. Hall decided to line the hand with inflatable air cells similar to those in pump sneakers.

It had to have a wrist that would cock when Larry went into his back swing.

Hall took his design to the owner of a Houston prosthetic company. The company was able to make the air cells all right, but the artificial wrist presented a problem. Then the owner discovered a prosthetic knee device made for a small child. The aluminum joint made a perfect wrist.

Larry got his new hand at Christmas time. He spent two months adjusting the prosthesis, then went out to practice his golf swing. His first drive went 200 yards.

A month after his high-school graduation, Larry again entered the Rancho Mirage tournament, and finished two strokes under his score for the previous year.

He went on to become a member of the golf team at Sam Houston State University.[2]

YOU HAVE FLEXIBILITY

So be sure that a situation is truly beyond your control before moving it out of your area of effective influence. And remember that while circumstances may be unchangeable, you have a great deal of flexibility in responding to circumstances. Major Franks never got his leg back and Larry Alford didn't get his hand back. But each responded proactively to the circumstances and found ways to deal with them effectively.

As you perform your situational triage, you'll make an interesting discovery: *The more you operate within your area of effective influence, the larger the area becomes.*

The principle that success begets success is a valid one. Each challenge that you meet and surmount opens new challenges for you and strengthens you to meet those challenges.

Successful people have learned to establish a pattern of successful action. Succeeding in small things builds confidence and creates an expectation of success that becomes a self-fulfilling prophecy.

So look for small ways to exert positive influence. Pick the challenges you know you can win.

Think of your life as a baseball season. Each time you come to the plate is an opportunity to get on base. Getting on base opens the opportunity to score a run. Each run scored takes you closer to victory in the ball game. Each victory enhances your opportunity to win the pennant. Winning the pennant opens the opportunity of getting into the World Series. And if you don't make it this year, there's always next year.

So find yourself a core motivation, built around a set of positive principles that are important to you. Identify your area of effective influence and let those principles motivate you and guide your actions. Identify the things you can change and go about changing them. Identify the things you can't change and develop positive strategies for dealing with them. Ignore the trivial. As H. Jackson Brown put it in his **_Life's Little Instruction Book_**, "Don't stop the parade to pick up a dime."

Stairway To Success

Prelude to Step Two

Make a Commitment

*Concerning all acts of initiative and cre-
ation, there is one elementary truth — that
the moment one definitely commits oneself,
then providence moves, too.*

— Goethe

Every salesperson knows the difference
between a decision and a commitment. A decision is
when the prospect says "Yes, I'll buy what you're selling." A commitment is when you have a signature on
a contract and a check in hand. Salespeople know not
to count on their commissions until they have the
commitments.

It's the same way in your personal life. Making
a decision is one thing; making a commitment is quite
another.

Many people go through life making decisions but dancing around their commitments. They're like the suitor who keeps saying "I'm going to marry you" but refuses to set the date.

Life is too important to be approached without commitment. If you want to control your destiny, you must be willing to make a decision on what you want and to make a commitment to achieve it.

To make a successful commitment, you need to do these things:

1. *Say good-bye to the past.*
2. *Create your future.*
3. *Cross your Rubicon.*

You can't take charge of your life without an awareness of where you've been, where you are, and where you're going. But you can't build your life on the past. The past is gone. Nor can you allow your destiny to be limited by present circumstances. The present is fleeting. The only place left to build your life is in the future.

You can let the future happen, or you can create it. You create it by forming a clear, vivid picture of what you want and fixing your mental and emotional eyes on that picture. Let it become your dream, and it will draw you toward the fulfillment.

You can't begin building your dream in earnest until you've crossed your Rubicon. To cross your Rubicon means to take a step from which there is no turning back. The expression is based on the actions of Julius Caesar when he was in command of a provincial Roman army. He knew that Roman law forbade him to lead his army outside its assigned province.

But Caesar wanted more than a provincial command. He wanted to rule the empire.

The boundary of his province was the River Rubicon. He knew that if he crossed the Rubicon he would have no choice but to continue on to Rome and conquer or be conquered. Caesar crossed the Rubicon, and the rest is history.

To seal your commitment and march successfully into the future, you have to cross your Rubicon. The future is a place you've never been before, and many people are a little nervous about entering it. They prefer the safe, familiar circum-stances of the past. But if you are trying constantly to relive the familiar past, you'll never enjoy the rewarding future.

The way to keep from reliving the past is to take that irrevocable step. Cut yourself off from past circumstances so that your only choice is to move ahead.

When you move with that kind of commitment, as Goethe said, providence moves too. You will find all kinds of ways to make the dream you created come true.

Chapter Five

Say Good-bye to the Past

The past is a bucket of ashes.

— Carl Sandburg

The past is over. Enjoy the good memories, use the bad ones as lessons in life, and get ready to make some new ones. Your focus should be on the future.

Imagine that you're the batter in a baseball game, waiting for the next pitch.

Think of the ball as your life and the path of the pitch as the course of time.

From the time the ball leaves the pitcher's hand until it passes over the plate, it is beyond your influence. It's in the future, out of reach.

The future becomes the present the split-second the ball crosses the plate. You can swing at it or you can let it go by. But as soon as the ball makes contact with the bat or pops into the catcher's mitt, you've lost control of it again. It's in the past. You may knock it into the stands, hit into a double play, strike out or walk. But your only chance to control what happens is in that minute speck of time when the ball is over the plate.

The future races toward the present, then zips into the past quicker than a 98-mile-per-hour fastball travels from the pitcher's mound to home plate.

If you decide not to commit yourself and swing, your fate is in the hands of the umpire. He can call a ball or a strike. If you swing, you take a risk, but you also step up to a scoring opportunity. And the outcome is in your hands.

VISUALIZE SUCCESS

Fortunately, life keeps throwing pitches at you. You get a chance to swing again and again. And though the future is out of your reach, you can always make use of the present to *prepare* for the future.

If you go up to the plate thinking about the double play you hit into the last time around, you'll probably be struck out or thrown out again.

But if, while you're in the on-deck circle, you visualize yourself making the perfect swing at the perfect pitch and knocking it out of the park, you're much more likely to have a successful turn at bat.

This is not speculation. It's a proven reality: People who *visualize* themselves doing what they want to do precisely the way they want to do it usually succeed at what they're trying. Their minds are in the present, but they're rehearsing for the future so that when it arrives their response systems will know what to do.

WELCOME CHANGE

Many people, though, are unable to rehearse for the future because they're too busy rehearsing the past.

So the first thing you have to do if you want to commit yourself to a dream is to ditch the past.

This means *seeking, accepting and embracing change*. If you want your future to be an improvement over your past, you have to be willing to give up the past and replace it with the future you want.

For many people, change is more threatening than challenging. They see it as the destroyer of what is familiar and comfortable rather than the creator of what is new and exciting.

But these days, if you don't change, you stagnate and die.

THE COCKPIT VS. THE PARACHUTE

A naval aviator once made an observation to me that illustrates the point.

He said many pilots have died because they stayed with their disabled aircraft too long. They preferred the familiarity of the cockpit to the unfamiliarity of the parachute, even though the cockpit had become a death trap.

Many people have seen their careers crash because they preferred the familiar but deadly old ways to the risky but rewarding new ways. They never learned that to stand pat is to go to pot.

PREPARING FOR CHANGE

If you prefer either the *accommodating* or *meticulous* behavioral mode, you are naturally wary of change. It makes you feel tense and uneasy. The *accommodating* person likes a smooth, undisturbed routine. The *meticulous* person likes for things to take place systematically, and therefore resents anything that causes a variation from the norm.

If you prefer either of those modes, you can prepare yourself for change. Remember that no matter how sweeping the changes, some things always remain the same.

TRAVELING THROUGH TIME

One way to prepare yourself is to engage in time travel. It's done all the time, you know. You have been traveling in time ever since you were born. You've just never found a way to control the pace or to reverse the direction.

Suppose you could do both. Imagine yourself at some earlier time of life. Now imagine what it would be like if you suddenly moved forward from that time to the present, like someone going "back to the future."

What contrasts would you observe between the past and the present? What similarities would you find?

When I first came to the United States, it was 1966. A lot has changed since then. We have VCRs and giant-screen television in our homes. Instead of two or three television channels for each market, we have a wide variety of choices through cable and satellite dishes. The kids spend hours playing computer games, and adults spend an increasing portion of their time in front of computer screens, through which they have access to individuals and data bases around the world. Available jobs require new skills and knowledge. It's a different world today, in many respects, from the one I found when I first came to America from the Middle East, a stranger to the people, the culture and the language.

But as I think back, many things are still the same. In 1966, all the young people wanted to own Ford Mustangs or Chevrolet Camaros. As I write this, the Mustang and Camaro are still competing vigorously for the sporty end of the automotive market, and although you see more Japanese name plates on cars in America, the majority of vehicles still bear names like Chevrolet, Ford, Plymouth, Dodge and Buick.

Jet air travel was popular in 1966. Many of today's airplanes are bigger, but they're not much faster.

Teen-agers spent hours talking to each other on the telephone. They still do.

People in my home town read the <u>High Point Enterprise</u> and stayed up for the 11 o'clock news on WGHPiedmont, the local television station. They still do.

Sports fans hung on every pitch in the World Series, followed the fortunes of their favorite professional football teams, cheered on their college heroes in the New Years' Day bowl games, followed the action in the NCAA basketball tournament. They still do. And the teams that show up regularly in these events are the teams I remember from the '60s: the Cowboys and Redskins; the Pirates and Braves; Notre Dame and Alabama; North Carolina and Kentucky.

Americans were in love with hamburgers and French fries, pizza and milk shakes. They still are.

Many of the singing voices we heard on LP and stereo records in 1966 still come to us via compact discs today, and many of the figures on movie and television screens then are readily recognized today. For years to come, Americans will be entertained by Frank Sinatra, Julie Andrews, Bob Hope, Carol Burnette, Andy Griffith, Dick Van Dyke, and Mary Tyler Moore — either in person or in re-runs.

My point is that, despite three decades of the fastest change in the history of the world, much remains the same. The person who went into hibernation in 1966 and awoke in the middle of the '90s would not step out into a totally new world.

So as you think about creating your own future, remember that you don't have to recreate a totally new world. Concentrate on the things that will remain familiar to you.

CULTIVATE AWARENESS

But if you want your future to be exciting and stimulating, you should also cultivate an awareness of exciting possibilities.

Do some mental time traveling. Imagine yourself in the future. Think about the way you would want it to be if you could have it any way you wanted it. Imagine the sights, sounds and smells of your future life. Become familiar with your dream, and when it arrives you won't be a total stranger to events.

Many people stay in ruts and make no effort to get out. It's not that they like the ruts; they just don't see any good reason to make the effort to get out.

You may be in a rut without knowing it. Here are some questions to serve as a reality check:

- ♦ When you think of your career, do you say, "Whatever the company wants me to do, I can do?"

- Do you go down every road that opens up, hoping it will lead to something bigger and better?

- Do you frequently wish you were doing something else at the moment, and keep promising yourself that some day it will be different?

- Do you stay busy most of the time doing things that seem urgent, but at the end of the day feel as though you haven't accomplished much?

- Do you feel that you've been fairly successful, but wonder whether you're doing the right things to reach your full potential?

- Do you avoid new methods because the old ones still work and the new ones may upset the routine?

- Do you base you future plans on the assumption that present trends will hold up for the future?

- Do you look upon change as a threat instead of as an opportunity?

If you answered "yes" to two or more of these questions, you may be drifting along in a rut, taking no responsibility for the direction of your life.

PAIN AND REWARD AS MOTIVATORS

If you're in a rut, you can use two motivational factors to energize you to get out: Pain and reward.

You may not like to get out of bed in the morning. But you do, because the pain of losing your job is greater than the pain of throwing off the covers and climbing out.

If your flight to Acapulco were leaving at 7 a.m., though, you would have no trouble getting out of bed, because the anticipation of pleasure would outweigh the pain of throwing back the covers.

You may not want to go to the dentist, but the pain of a tooth ache is greater than the pain of the drill.

You endure the agony of a steep mountain climb because of the breathtaking view that awaits you at the top.

Put pain and pleasure to work in motivating you toward change. When you decide that you don't want your future to be a repetition of your past, think of all the things you dislike about your present circumstances. Dwell on the pain and aggravation they cause you. Then visualize the pleasures that would accompany constructive change. Associating pleasure with change and pain with the rut will help energize you toward a commitment to change.

Look at change the way you look at a pool of water just before you jump in. You know that there's going to be a shock when your body leaves the warmth of the air and feels the cool water. But you know that your body will adjust quickly and you'll enjoy the pleasure of swimming and floating and splashing.

A TASTE FOR NEW EXPERIENCES

You can cultivate a taste for stimulating new experiences if you're willing to take the plunge.

If you're in the habit of having lunch at the same meat-and-potatoes restaurant time after time, break the pattern once in a while. Try a Chinese, Japanese, Lebanese, Thai or Vietnamese restaurant for a change. You may find something you really like. Imagine what life would be like if you had never taken the trouble to taste a pineapple or banana, a pizza or an egg roll for the first time.

If you've been spending your vacation at the seashore or the mountains every year, try something different. Visit a foreign country if your budget will allow it. French-speaking Quebec is just across the border from New York and New England. Spanish-speaking Mexico is a relatively short drive from California's Disneyland, just across town from El Paso and Laredo, and a pleasant cruise away from Miami. Europe is closer to New York City than Los Angeles is.

"Travel has a way of stretching the mind," wrote Ralph Cranshaw in the _Journal of the American Medical Association_. "The stretch comes not from travel's immediate rewards, the inevitable myriad new sights, smells and sounds, but with experiencing firsthand how others do differently what we have believed to be the right and only way.

Author Robert Louis Stevenson adds: "If you can't travel, read about new places." Your public library will have illustrated books on other places, and probably a number of videotapes as well.

Expand your tastes in music, art and entertainment. Your new knowledge will give you a great deal more self-confidence, which will help you in coping with change.

In social situations, learn to take the initiative. If you're at a party, go up to a stranger, introduce yourself and start a conversation. It will be easier if you've read a good book, seen a good movie or learned something new from newspaper and television reports. But you don't have to be a fountain of information to start a conversation. Learn to ask open-ended questions that give the strangers an opportunity to talk and tell you about themselves.

The point of all this is to transform yourself gradually into a broader, more flexible and more adaptable person — the kind who can deal comfortably with new things and who won't have to use old ways as a crutch.

MAKING CHANGE THE NORM

You'll find change less upsetting if you learn to look upon it as the norm — as indeed it is.

Make it a habit to go about every day looking for things that you can change for the better. It may be something as simple as a minor change of routine. It may be a new hair style or a new approach to your wardrobe. It may be a different route to work.

One rule of thumb holds that when you've done something the same way for at least two years, there's probably a better way of doing it.

Playwright George Bernard Shaw lived in an age when the pace of change was slower. But he was always examining new ideas.

"It is an instinct with me personally," he said, "to attack every idea which has been full grown for 10 years."

If you don't learn to move with change, you'll soon find the world moving ahead while you lag behind.

Here's an exercise to help you determine your openness to change:

List three major changes that have occurred in your life during the past five years. Then answer these questions:

1. Did you initiate any of these changes?

2. If you didn't initiate them, did you antici-pate them, or did they take you by surprise?

3. In what ways did you change your behavior in response to these changes

4. Did you resist these changes or welcome them?

5. What future changes do you anticipate, and how do you expect to deal with them?

If you just drifted into these changes without initiating them, and dealt with them by following the course of least resistance, you need to acquire the tools of CHANGE.

These tools are necessary if you want to control the changes in your life:

Creativity.
Healthy habits.
Accommodation.
Nose for news.
Good bye to the past.
Eagerness to succeed.

CREATIVITY

Change can be confronted with an air of resignation or of challenge. If you accept it with resignation, you're at the mercy of change. If you accept it as a challenge, change is your creative instrument.

Creativity is often assumed to be an inborn trait, but it can be learned.

Your creative energies often can be ignited by a two-word question: *What next?*

What next? puts the ball in the future's court, and it calls for change. It keeps you from being married to an unproductive idea. You say, "This isn't working; *what next?*" and immediately your mind begins searching for another solution. It lets you build on your experiences:

"This method is an improvement over the last one, but it isn't quite what I'm looking for. *What next?*"

"I can see now why that procedure didn't work. *What next?*"

Knowledge is to creativity what a bed of coals is to a fire. It provides a reservoir of resources to keep the creative fires burning. So to develop creativity, acquire a thirst for knowledge. Read, travel and explore. Browse through libraries, book stores, and magazine racks. Savor new places and new experiences. Share your knowledge with other people and ask them to share theirs with you. Don't be afraid to use borrowed ideas and borrowed methods. Be open to innovative thinking and innovative procedures, regardless of where they originate.

HEALTHY HABITS

Change is challenging, stressful and often uncomfortable. To deal with it successfully, you need to be healthy in body and mind.

Physical fitness therefore is an important asset for anyone coping with change. It gives you both physical and emotional energy.

Good communication with peers is a source of emotional strength for dealing with change. You'll feel better when you're able to talk over your challenges and opportunities with people who understand them and who sympathize with you.

Set aside time to think about the changes you anticipate. If you understand the causes and probable effects of the changes, you'll be in better position to deal with them.

Keep your perspective. As I mentioned earlier, although changes are happening around you, some things will remain familiar and stable. Take a balanced approach. Confront the challenges, but find time to enjoy yourself too.

Cultivate a sense of humor. Humor is the pleasant lubricant of life. If you approach change with a sense of humor, you'll take the sharp edges off the adjustments and smooth the way for you and those around you. As Marianne Moore put it, "Humor saves a few steps, it saves years."

And as Shakespeare wrote: "They laugh that win."

ACCOMMODATION

You can't deal with change by resisting it. You have to accommodate it.

A wise Danish king who once ruled England taught this lesson to his followers by going down to the seashore and demonstrating that he, powerful ruler that he was, could not stop the tide from coming in.

Change is just as inevitable as the tide. Don't try to stop it. Accommodate it, channel it, and use it, but don't try to stop it. And just as one wave is surely followed by another, so one change is followed by another change. You can't accommodate one change and then relax. You have to get ready for the next one.

Remember too that change brings opportunity. You'll miss out on the opportunity if you tackle next year's problems with the methods that worked last year. You won't recognize the possibilities in the future if you assume that the future will be no more than the past with a face lift. Base your planning on change, not on the status quo. Your most frequently used tool should be your imagination, not your memory.

NOSE FOR NEWS

If you're going to deal with change, you'll have to keep up with change. You can't adjust to what you don't know. So it's important to read extensively the literature dealing with the field in which you pursue success. Attend seminars where the latest trends are discussed. Use video and audio tapes to keep you updated on events and trends. Keep an eye out for changes that will affect your life. Think about ways these changes will affect you and how you will respond to them.

GOOD BYE TO THE PAST

When you decide to buy all new furniture for your home, what do you have to do?

You probably have to get rid of most of your old furniture. Otherwise, there won't be room for the new.

The same thing is true of new ideas and new ways of doing things. Before you can make significant changes, you have to get rid of the old ways. You have to let go of the ideas and habits you've grown comfortable with. You have to forget old resentments and old grudges.

EAGERNESS TO SUCCEED

If you expect change to be a downer, it's probably going to be a downer. If you expect it to result in better things, it's probably going to result in better things. Events, like people, usually live up to your expectations. So one of the most powerful tools you can take into the era of change is a positive attitude — an expectation that whatever changes are taking place, you're going to ride them to success.

Your value to your family, your company and your community will depend upon your reaction to change. You can't be a leader if you don't keep up with change. Therefore, it's important that you monitor the way change affects you at a personal level.

One way of monitoring the effects of change is to keep a journal. Periodically, take the time to summarize in your journal the things that are changing in your life and the way you're responding to them. If you find yourself feeling anxious or frustrated, decide what needs to be done to remove these negative feelings. Then take action immediately.

Successful people are always living for new beginnings. As H.G. Wells wrote, "Life begins perpetually." Living for the future is the best way to build pleasant memories. Enjoy those memories, and keep producing more of them. The past can be a wonderful place to visit, but you wouldn't want to live there.

Chapter Six

Create Your Future

Destiny is not a matter of chance, it is a matter of choice; it is not a thing to be waited for, it is a thing to be achieved.

— William Jennings Bryan

A decision is made with the brain. A commitment is made with the heart. Therefore, a commitment is much deeper and more binding than a decision.

Commitment involves feeling as well as thinking. It is the result of a well-documented formula: Thoughts plus feelings equal action.

Everything you do has to be born in the brain as an idea. That idea gives birth to a feeling. You act on the basis of the feeling. Therefore, your actions turn your thoughts into reality, once you have been motivated by your feelings.

The deeper and more intense your feelings, the more powerful the motivation to turn thoughts into action.

The thought creates an image. The feeling makes the image glow. Action brings the image to life.

Your vision is created in your mind. When you think about it, feel deeply about it, and act in harmony with it, your vision will guide you to success.

Figure 6-1

THE VISIONING PROCESS

The process I have just described is what we know as *visioning*. It is the process of *creating your future*.

Many people go through life unaware that this creative power lies within them. Yet we all have it. You can create the future you want. It's all a matter of forming a vision, committing yourself to that vision, and acting in harmony with the vision.

The power of visioning has been statistically demonstrated. Harvard University once surveyed a class of its alumni over a 20-year period to learn what distinguished the successful ones from the unsuccessful.

It found that 97% of the wealth of that class was concentrated in only 3% of its members. The ultra-successful 3% had one thing in common: All of them were clear about their goals, had written them down, and had reviewed them daily.

Goals are simply a way of breaking a vision into doable units.

Your vision should involve much more than your career. It should encompass all areas of your life. Many people create visions for their careers, their families, and their physical, spiritual, emotional and social lives. All these components together constitute a holistic vision.

MAKING THE VISION GLOW

You learned in Step One how to decide what you want in life, based on your talents, your values-based principles, and your preferred behavioral mode.

Now you need to make those desires glow by forming them into a vision. Then you need to translate that vision into a written mission statement. Next, divide it into achievable goals.

How do you make the vision glow?

First, the vision must involve a future that excites you. It must be something you desire passionately. You must want it so much you can see it, feel it, smell it and taste it.

A VISION ON KILLINGTON PEAK

That must have been the way Preston Smith felt when he first stood on Killington Peak in Vermont and envisioned a ski resort there. Though the reality was yet in the future, he must have smelled the cold scent of the wind blowing off the forested slopes; seen the pattern of sunlight and shadow on the ski trails; heard the shouts of skiers calling to each other as they rode the ski-lift to the top; heard the screams of novices taking their first spills on the beginners' slopes; felt the warmth from burning logs crackling in an open fireplace while the sun sank into its nest of splendor behind the Green Mountains.

USE BOTH SIDES OF YOUR BRAIN

Can you see a vivid picture of yourself in the future you desire?

It may be hard to do while you're sitting behind a desk, grinding away at your work station, or pounding the streets looking for work. When you're occupied in this manner, your left brain is fully engaged.

Your left brain is the logical, decision-making side of your mind. Your right brain is the intuitive, creative side. To create your future, you need to form an image in your right brain, then use your left brain to turn the image into reality.

All of us use both sides of our brains. But in most of us, one side is dominant. The side of the brain that you use the most determines whether you are basically a logical or a creative person. Successful people can be found in both categories. High achievers learn to integrate the creative and the logical sides of their brains.

The left brain is more disciplined than the right. It can absorb information, organize it, compare one fact with another, and reason step by step.

When Preston Smith stood on Killington Peak and dreamed of his ski resort, he viewed it through the right side of his brain. But when he began to map out a strategy for achieving the dream, he turned to his left brain.

We can hear him saying, "If I'm going to build a ski resort here, I must first negotiate a lease on the land. Then I'll need to get financial backing. Next I'll have to persuade the state to build a road into the area. To guarantee success, I'll need to find a reliable way to keep an acceptable amount of snow on the slopes."

That was Smith's left brain at work.

The right brain is more freewheeling. It daydreams. It focuses on the forest instead of the trees. It looks at possibilities instead of realities. The left brain is interested in the world as it is. The right brain is interested in the world as it might be. The left brain relies on facts. The right brain trusts its intuition. The left brain is anchored in the here and now. The right brain vaults into the future.

The right brain is the source of ideas.

The left brain is the source of plans.

GETTING INTO YOUR RIGHT BRAIN

So to begin the visioning process, you need to get into your right brain. There's no magic to it. You do it all the time. Have you ever wrestled with a knotty problem all day, then decided to "sleep on it." And as you were drifting into sleep or waking from a night's rest, did the solution pop into your head?

When you're going to sleep, your mind relaxes. The left brain surrenders its dominance, and the right brain takes over. This is when you're at your most creative. Your right brain pans your storehouse of knowledge and experiences, like a flashlight beam passing over the contents of your attic. When it comes across the right gem of information for the problem you're seeking to resolve, or the stored-away idea that is just right for your purposes, the gem lights up, like a jewel reflecting the flashlight rays. A light comes on in your conscious mind.

So to create your future, find some time when you can relax your body and your mind. You may want to retreat to a hideaway by the lake or seashore or up in the mountains. Or you may have a favorite nook at home where you can relax and get comfortable. You may even be able to relax, with your feet up, in the privacy of your office.

Let your mind wander. Don't try to concentrate. Just relax and get in touch with your deepest values and your strongest desires. What would you want to do if anything were possible? Picture your ideal world, and put yourself there.

For some people, dreaming is like watching a movie. They're in front of a screen viewing the action. The most vivid dreamers are able to put themselves on the screen. They're actually experiencing the environment and the action.

Let your thoughts take you into the future without worrying about where you are now. Remember, you're creating the future, not remodeling the past.

As Carl Jung, the renowned behaviorist, noted, "Without this playing with fantasy no creative work has ever yet come to birth."

SETTING UP A FORCE FIELD

When you vividly picture the future the way you want it to be, you set up a powerful force field that draws you toward the fulfillment of the vision.

Your subconscious mind — the seat of your motivation — doesn't distinguish between reality and perception. It believes what the conscious mind tells it. So when you consciously envision your desired future, seeing yourself in the role you want to play, your subconscious mind sees this as reality. It motivates you to act in harmony with this perceived reality. And your actions turn the dream into actuality.

Begin the creation of your vision by asking these questions while you're in a peaceful, relaxed state:

◆ What am I passionate about?

◆ What makes life worth living?

◆ What do I desire most strongly?

Then form a vivid picture of the things you desire.

BYPASS YOUR CIRCUMSTANCES

Don't limit yourself to the things you think are achievable, given your present circumstances. If you're hungry, you want food, regardless of whether there's anything to eat near at hand. Your hunger will focus your mental and physical faculties on the task of finding food — and you'll probably find it. Think of the times when you've wanted to buy something but didn't have the money. If you wanted it badly enough, you *found* the money, one way or another.

It's that way with a vision. Without a glowing vision, you'll regard your desirable future as unattainable, and you won't focus your efforts on attaining it. You will be imprisoned by your circumstances.

"Man is not a creature of circumstances," said British statesman Benjamin Disraeli. "Circumstances are the creatures of men."

A vision bypasses circumstances. It finds a way around them, over them or under them. Or it rearranges the circumstances. One way or another, it will take you toward your objectives.

Many people form visions for each aspect of their lives. They have visions for their families, visions for their careers, and visions for their social lives. These visions, of course, must complement each other, or their lives will be out of focus.

CREATE A MISSION STATEMENT

After you've created your vision, you need to keep it in front of you at all times. To do this, it helps to have a mission statement.

Your mission statement translates your vision into words. It tells why you are here and what you propose to do with your life.

Your mission statement should be brief and simple. It is more powerful when it is expressed in the present tense. Describe your vision as if you had already achieved it.

If your career vision calls for you to become the president of your own company, state it as if you were already in the CEO's chair: "I am the president of a software company. My office is in Carmel, California, overlooking the Pacific. . ."

Your vision gains power when you go public with it. Let your friends and associates know what you expect to achieve. When you put your commitment on record, you're giving yourself an extra incentive to succeed. Perhaps the most famous home run in baseball history was struck by Babe Ruth after he had taken two strikes, then pointed to the outfield fence. On the next pitch, Babe sent the ball flying into the section of the stands where he had pointed. Imagine how he would have felt had he struck out. Babe had given himself a task, and had gone public with it before thousands of fans. He now had all the more reason to accomplish what he set out to accomplish.

A copy of your mission statement, framed and displayed in a prominent place, can be a constant reminder for you, your family and your associates of the commitment you have made. Your subconscious mind will adopt the vision and will constantly direct your behavior toward achieving it.

SOMETHING YOU PASSIONATELY DESIRE

Your vision can't be a half-hearted thing. It must be something you passionately desire, and it must represent something you believe you can attain. But it also must be something that will inspire you to rise to the best of your ability.

Many people deny themselves the pleasure of living life to the fullest because they follow limited visions. They dream modest dreams, so they compile modest achievements. The limiting factor is not their capacity to achieve but their willingness to believe in themselves.

Don't let self-doubt stand between you and what you desire. You can achieve what you want to achieve, provided you believe in yourself. And provided you have faith in God.

Roman Emperor Marcus Aurelius put it this way, freely translated:

> Don't think that what is hard for you to master is impossible for man; but if a thing is possible and proper to man, consider it attainable by you.

In Chapter 12, we discuss ways to achieve the self-confidence you need to create and fulfill an ambitious vision.

Your successful future is waiting to be created. Get in touch with your values, your principles and your desires. Then use your powerful mind to create the future you want. I'm convinced that our Creator wants us to achieve our fullest potential. Not for selfish fulfillment but so we can serve others. The highest order of success, to me, is to love others and help them however I can.

Chapter Seven

Cross Your Rubicon

Nothing resists a human will that stakes its very existence upon the achievement of its purpose.

—Benjamin Disraeli

Once you've created your vision of the future, you seal the commitment by crossing your Rubicon and bidding good-bye to the past.

You are invading new territory — the territory of the future. You're no longer going to be bound by the circumstances of the past.

RE-ENGINEER YOUR LIFE

Many successful people have turned their backs on the past by embarking on the individual equivalent of "re-engineering the corporation."

When corporate leaders decide to re-engineer the corporation, they don't just set out to improve the present system. They set out to create an entirely new system.

When you set out to re-engineer your life, you're not just improving your present circumstances. You're creating a whole new set of circumstances, in keeping with your vision of what life should be.

THE CATERPILLAR BECOMES A BUTTERFLY

__Harvard Business Review__ compares it with the metamorphosis of a caterpillar into a butterfly.

"A butterfly is not more caterpillar or a better or improved caterpillar; a butterfly is a different creature," noted authors Tracy Goss, Richard Pascale, and Anthony Athos[1].

Becoming the butterfly you want to be means putting the old circumstances in the past, and concentrating all your resources on creating the new ones.

This can be risky and scary. You're leaving the comfort and security of the old cocoon and accepting the challenges and uncertainties of a free environment. It's natural to want to leave the path open for a return to the old ways if the new ways don't work out.

But if you leave the path open, you're quite likely to retrace it. At the first sign of adversity, you'll give up the adventure and return to your cocoon — the life you were trying to put behind.

A butterfly, of course, cannot return to its cocoon. The moment it makes its way to the outside and flutters its wings, it is committed to a new type of existence. Its life as a butterfly is not just a matter of what it *does*. It is also a matter of what it *is*.

TRANSFORMING YOURSELF

You can shut off the path to retreat by transforming yourself into something you never were before.

The process of education can be transforming. Oliver Wendell Holmes Sr. wrote that when a mind stretches to embrace a new idea, it "never shrinks back to its original dimensions." There is a qualitative difference between an educated person and an uneducated person, just as there is a qualitative difference between a butterfly and a caterpillar. Acquire an education and you have crossed an important Rubicon.

Acquiring the mindset of a professional is another way of fording the Rubicon. As Bernard De Voto observed:

> *Between the amateur and the professional . . .there is a difference not only in degree but in kind. The skillful man is, within the function of his skill, a different integration, a different nervous and muscular and psychological organization.*

You can follow a professional or a worker mentality. Being a professional involves far more than acquiring skill. It involves acquiring a whole new mindset.

The worker mentality sees a job as a necessary evil that has to be endured until quitting time sets you free to pursue your *real* life. Professionals see their careers as rewarding *components* of their real lives. They learn to integrate their careers and their personal lives so that one meshes with and supports the other.

Workers wait for someone to tell them what to do and how to do it, and they let others worry about whether the way they're told to do it is the right way. They may concentrate on performing their assigned tasks well, but won't worry about what happens outside their own areas.

Professionals take responsibility for their own success and for the success of the organizations to which they belong. They see themselves as partners in prosperity with the organization, and see the organization's ups and downs as their own. They are constantly looking for things that they personally can do to contribute to organizational success.

Workers accept a ceiling on success in return for a steady income. They are not boat-rockers, but believe in doing things the way they've always been done — which they perceive as the safe, cautious way.

Professionals are willing to take intelligent risks, accepting the possibility of failure as a fair price for the opportunity to grow.

Workers concentrate on the means. They do their jobs without worrying about how their jobs contribute to the total picture.

Professionals concentrate on the ends. They see their jobs in terms of how they contribute to the organization's success.

Professionals are usually perceived as good because they go the extra mile to *be* good. They keep up with the latest developments in their field, and share their knowledge with others. They communicate confidence, dressing and grooming themselves for success and always conscious of the importance of image.

To achieve this type of professionalism, you must set a high standard for yourself and never allow yourself to fall below that standard.

Acquiring manners, culture and good taste also transforms. These qualities mark you as a cultured person, one that successful people will respect and admire. Once you have acquired professional and cultural polish, you have become a different person, and you won't go back to what you were before.

ACTION IS REQUIRED

But crossing your Rubicon involves *action* as well as *being*. Something has to happen that signals a dramatic break with the past. The butterfly has to crawl out of the cocoon. The uneducated person has to enroll in a course of study. Caesar has to give the order to advance beyond the river.

To commit yourself beyond turning back, you have to take decisive action. The moment you foreclose the possibility of going back, you will invoke the inner powers that will enable you to forge success in your new life.

"Be bold," urges author J. Jackson Brown Jr. "Providence loves boldness, and will assist you in ways you wouldn't imagine."

William Murray, a member of a Scottish expedition that climbed Mount Everest, expressed a similar view. When you make a commitment, he said:

> *All sorts of things occur to help one that would never have otherwise occurred. A whole stream of events issues from the decision, raising in one's favor all manner of unforeseen incidents and meetings and material assistance which no man could have ever dreamed would come his way.*

The knowledge that the only path open is the one ahead focuses your energy and resources and multiplies your chances of success.

COMMITMENT ON THE VOLGA

One of the great turning points in World War II was the Battle of Stalingrad (now Volgagrad), when the Russian army staked everything on the defense of the city.

Had the Germany army been able to cross the Volga River at that point, the Russian heartland would have been open to the Nazi advance.

The Russian Army stood on the west side of the Volga and made its stand. The word went out to the soldiers: *There is no other side of the river.*

That was commitment. The Russians fought as if there were no place to retreat. And the German tide was turned back.

NORMANDY VS. THE BAY OF PIGS

For Dwight Eisenhower, the Rubicon was the English Channel. Had the weather turned against him, he would be remembered as one of history's great losers. He could have hedged his bet by telling his aides: "Let's send the boys on their way, but if it looks too blustery to land, they can turn around and come back."

Such a half-hearted commitment almost certainly would have ended in disaster — the way it did at the Bay of Pigs.

In that fiasco, President John Kennedy gave the go-ahead for anti-Castro Cubans to launch a liberating attack on the island, promising to provide them with air cover. At the last moment, the president decided that overt American participation was too risky, so he withdrew the air cover. The landing failed and good men were sent to their deaths.

Later, Kennedy confronted Soviet Premier Nikita Khrushchev with his own Rubicon: Soviet ships would not be permitted to sail into Cuban waters with offensive missiles on board. Khrushchev decided to stay on his side of the river, much to the relief of the world.

YOU CAN'T BE TENTATIVE

It takes determination and confidence to cross the Rubicon and burn your bridges behind you. But until you take that step, everything you do has a tentative quality to it.

Successful parents know that they do their children no favors when they bail them out every time they get into financial difficulty. They know that children will never be able to achieve success on their own so long as they know the parents will rescue them from their mistakes. They have to strike out on their own, cutting themselves off from the security blanket of home and parents.

To learn to fly, a nestling has to get out of the nest and trust its wings to keep it from hitting the ground.

To learn to swim, you eventually have to take your feet off the bottom and trust the water to hold you up.

MAKE THE CLEAN BREAK

I'm not suggesting that you suddenly and impulsively quit your job, sell your assets, move across the continent and start a new life from square one.

That's not boldness; it's foolhardiness.

But if you plan to follow your vision to success, you have to make a clean break with the past and set your face resolutely toward the future.

If you take a leave of absence from your steady job to take on a career in real-estate sales, you're very likely to return to your job. You'll fail as a real-estate salesperson because you won't go the extra mile to cultivate the skills and knowledge necessary to succeed. Deep down, you'll know you've got a familiar job waiting for you if it doesn't work out. You'll keep your attention focused on the "other side of the river" — the familiar side that offers safety but little opportunity

You'll be going into real estate acknowledging the possibility of failure. Your subconscious will pick up on that idea, and will cause you to act like a failure when you attempt to sell real estate. As William Feather put it, "Success is seldom achieved by people who contemplate the possibility of failure."

DROP THE EXCUSES

Crossing your Rubicon means cutting yourself loose from all your excuses for inaction:

"I'd like to go into business for myself, but I hate to give up a secure job."

Cross your Rubicon. If your vision calls for opening your own business, be sure you have enough capital, information and know-how to get it started, then resign your job and commit yourself to your new enterprise. You'll never succeed until you've made up your mind to try.

"I'd like to learn computer science, but I don't have time for night classes because I had to take on a second job to pay for my boat."

If taking that computer science course is necessary to fulfilling your vision, cross your Rubicon. Sell the boat and quit your second job. With your new job skills, you may be able to buy another boat later without holding down two jobs — and that will give you the leisure to use the boat.

"I'd like to go into business on the West Coast, but I own a home here in the East, and I can't keep up two residences."

Cross your Rubicon. Sell your house in the East and move to the West Coast. They have houses for sale out there too. With no home to return to, you'll be more likely to stick it out on the West Coast until your new business is a going concern.

"That new outfit would look great on me if I lost 15 pounds, but I'm afraid I'd never stick to my diet."

Cross your Rubicon and buy the outfit. It'll provide you with an extra incentive to lose the weight.

Crossing the Rubicon involves risk, but risk-taking is an important ingredient in success.

"Security is mostly a superstition," said Helen Keller. "It does not exist in nature. Life is either a daring adventure or nothing."

Successful people don't avoid risks. They learn to manage them. They don't dive off cliffs into unexplored waters. They learn how deep the water is, and make sure there are no hidden obstacles. Then they plunge in.

The process of risk analysis is not that complicated. Before crossing your Rubicon, examine the venture and answer these questions:

> **(1)** What is the best thing that could happen as a result of this action?

> **(2)** What is the worst that could happen as a result of this action?

> **(3)** What is the most likely result of this action?

If the *most likely* result would take you toward your vision, and you're willing to deal with the *worst possible* result in exchange for a shot at the *best possible* result, go ahead and cross.

FROM HAIR COLORING TO PIZZA

The business world is full of examples of people who took a look at where they were and where they wanted to be, then crossed their Rubicons.

Michael K. Lorelli started out in the marketing department at Clairol after earning his master's degree in business administration at New York University. Within two years he became product manager, and he proved his mettle by leading the fight against the Food and Drug Administration's efforts to ban certain ingredients in Clairol's hair-coloring products. Lorelli's team demonstrated that the ingredients posed no credible health risks, and the FDA backed off. His future with Clairol seemed assured. But Lorelli's vision beckoned him beyond his marketing niche and toward higher management.

Playtex International approached him with an offer. The company wanted to go global, and it needed someone to spearhead the effort. Lorelli, then 36, was told, in effect: "If you can develop a strategy that excites us, we'll put you in charge of the new business; if you fail, you may not have a future with us."[2]

Lorelli crossed his Rubicon. He left Clairol and joined Playtex. He had to stretch beyond his marketing experience and skills to build manu-facturing plants, set up a distribution network, find sources for raw materials and form joint ventures and licensing agreements with other companies. Within a few years, his division was generating $100 million in revenue in 10 countries.

Lorelli found other Rubicons to cross. He left Playtex for Pepsico, where he went from senior vice president for marketing of Pepsi Cola to head of Pepsi Cola's eastern division in the United States. Then he moved to Pizza Hut, another Pepsico enterprise, which had 2,500 outlets in 84 countries, with the challenge of doubling the number of outlets by 1996.

Lorelli didn't dive blindly into strange waters. He estimated the risks, estimated his own capacity to grow, consulted his personal vision, and waded in.

TAKING A RISK FOR A CONGENIAL ROLE

Herbert Korthoff also found success on the other side of his Rubicon. As a child, he spent nine years in an orphanage, where he learned that "you have to take control of your own life, or someone will do it for you."

Korthoff was graduated from Syracuse University and went to work for American Home Products. During a decade with the company, he took night classes and earned a master's in business administration.

He became head of purchasing and manufacturing and was confident that he could become a division vice president by the time he retired.

But his career at American Home Products was not a *congenial role* for Korthoff. He considered himself a maverick, and didn't feel comfortable with the company's hierarchical management structure. When he was 35, he had an opportunity to join U.S. Surgical, a company that provided physicians with easy-to-use surgical staples. According to *Fortune* magazine, six executives had crashed trying to make U.S. Surgical's manufacturing operations efficient.

Korthoff accepted the challenge, and adopted a strategy that he called the "three R's of management" — respect, recognition and remuneration. Within a few years he had the factories running smoothly and moved on to new challenges.[3]

SWAPPING A HOME FOR AN EDUCATION

Lew Richfield had a successful career as assistant to the chairman of a $140 million company. But he regretted the fact that he had never gone to college, and he felt something was missing from his life.

At the age of 45, he volunteered to serve part-time at a suicide-prevention center and discovered that he had a talent for working with people.

At the age of 46, both he and his wife Gloria entered college. They sealed their commitment by selling their home to pay their way. Both earned Ph.D. degrees and became full-time family therapists. He has since written two books on aging and relationships.

As Richfield's friend, professional basketball coach Pat Riley, observed: "I'm convinced that all great breakthroughs in life happen because they deny the crippling fear of failure. So listen to the inner voice that counsels courage, that affirms your life and your ability, and you will tap the power that makes a winner."[4]

Many of my friends did it too. Joe Jacobs started a small engineering firm in the tough times of the 1930's and built it into a multi-billion-dollar consulting company respected the world over.

Casey Kasem catapulted a radio career from a single radio station in Detroit to becoming the star of several internationally syndicated programs including Casey's Top 40. Today, he's a member of the Radio Hall of Fame and a highly respected professional.

Tom Davis founded Piedmont Aviation with a few dollars and three employees. He built it into one of America's finest regional companies: Piedmont Airlines. Later, he merged it profitably with USAir.

All of them were determined to succeed. None were tentative. Each crossed his Rubicon with commitment and vision.

Stairway To Success

Prelude to Step Three

Getting from Here to There

You can never plan the future by the past.
—Edmund Burke.

You create your future by forming a vision and expressing it through a mission statement. Your dream now glitters on the horizon of the future. But you are standing in the reality of the here and now.

How do you close the gap between where you are now and where you want to be?

You can't dream your way into the future. You have to have a plan. You have to know where you want to go and decide how you're going to get there.

The important word here is "how." The word "if" won't take you there. To achieve your vision, you must approach it with a positive attitude —a sense of certainty that your dream is achievable. You must adopt the attitude of Hannibal, the great general from ancient Carthage, who asserted: "We will either find a way, or make one."

A plan will establish a route to your destination. It will also provide for the elimination of road-blocks and the blazing of new trails across uncharted territory. It will prevent you from drifting aimlessly through life. A good plan will have these characteristics:

- It will specify actions. A good plan is proactive. It specifies what actions you will take to bring your vision to reality. It puts you in control of events instead of forcing you to respond to events.

- It will set a timetable. Without a specific timetable, your plan loses cohesion and never gains momentum. Nothing gets accomplished "sooner or later." It gets accomplished at a specific time and specific place.

- It will be flexible. You can't anticipate every event and circumstance that might have an impact on your future, but you can allow for contingencies.

You formed your vision in the creative right side of your brain. To create a workable plan, you need to bring the left side of the brain into the picture. You'll still need the right brain to conceive of creative ideas. But you'll use your left brain to pass ultimate judgment on these ideas, to set priorities, and to devise workable action plans.

You begin the planning process by revisiting your vision and reviewing your mission statement. Assess your present circumstances and measure the gap between where you are and where you want to be. Then follow these steps:

1. Set goals.
2. Set priorities.
3. Develop strategies.

As you develop your plan, keep this point in mind: Your present circumstances do not control your options. They establish a starting point, but they don't determine your destination. Where you are very quickly becomes where you've been. So keep your eyes focused on the future — where you want to go — instead of on the past — where you've been.

Have a good trip.

Chapter Eight

Set Goals

---

*Nothing contributes so much to tranquilize
the mind as a steady purpose — a point on
which the soul may fix its intellectual eye.*

— Mary Wollstonecraft Shelley

Good personal planning involves no more than
determining how you will get from your present circumstances to the future you have created through
your vision.

The trouble with many plans is that they are
based on the way things are now. To be successful,
your personal plan must focus on what you want, not
what you have.

If you focus on what you have, your future will be limited by your present circumstances. If you focus on what you want, your imagination will be set free to explore the possibilities.

ONE STEP AT A TIME

Suppose you live in rural Kansas and you have a burning desire to see the sights of a big city. But you look around you and all you see is farmland. If you focus on present circumstances, you'll say, "Well, I guess I'll just have to learn to like farms and ranches. That's all we have around here."

But in reality, you're not a prisoner of circumstances. You don't *have* to be tied to your farm in Kansas. You are in the geographic center of the continental United States. You can travel north to Minneapolis-St. Paul, west to Los Angeles or east to Washington, D.C. Your present circumstances don't determine where you can go; they merely determine where you start.

Suppose you want to see Los Angeles.

"That's half a continent away," you tell yourself, "and I live out in the country, miles from nowhere. How can I get there from here?"

You don't get there in a single leap. You break the trip down into steps. You get in your car (or pickup truck) and you drive into Topeka or to Kansas City. You buy an airline ticket. You board a plane. Before you can say "San Fernando Valley," you're descending to Los Angeles International Airport.

So you don't have the money? Start a savings account.

Don't have a job? Find one.

Don't have the qualifications? Get them.

In moving toward your personal vision, you don't do everything at once. It's like moving a huge pile of stones. You don't pick up the whole pile and carry it to the new location. You move it a rock at a time, just as you go from Kansas to California one step at a time.

So the task of fulfilling your personal vision involves figuring out what steps you need to take and when to take them.

BREAKING YOUR MISSION INTO DOABLE CHUNKS

In life, this is known as goal-setting.

You break your personal mission into doable chunks, and you do them one at a time. You determine where you want to go and what you want to be. You identify the milestones you need to pass on the way. And you make those milestones your goals.

Notice that in setting the goals to take you from Kansas to California, you don't start from Kansas. You start from California. You envision yourself landing at LA International. That means you'll have to buy a plane ticket. A plane ticket will require money. Money will require a job. A job will require qualifications. If you say "I need job qualifications," before you say "I want to go to California," your efforts will not be

143

focused. You won't know the end result you're seeking, and so you won't have firm guidance in deciding what qualifications to acquire and what job to accept. You will end up taking whatever job comes along and going wherever that job permits you to go — which may be downtown Topeka. You will become a *prisoner* of circumstances rather than a *creator* of circumstances.

YOUR PRESENT REALITY

PLAN BACKWARD FROM THE VISION

So begin your planning with your personal vision in mind. Decide what you want to achieve. Decide when you want to achieve it. Then plan backward in time to the present.

Your vision represents your overall objective in life. You won't achieve it in a day, probably not in a year, and perhaps not in a decade. But you want to make steady, measurable progress toward your vision.

You make that progress by setting and achieving definite goals. Effective planning involves four types of goals: long-range, medium-range, short-range, and immediate.

Long-range goals are broad objectives that will require several years to achieve. They may have deadlines 10, 15 or even 20 years in the future. Medium-range goals are more specific. They specify the things you need to accomplish to achieve long-range goals. Usually, they involve time frames of one to five years.

Short-term goals usually encompass time periods of less than a year. They tell you what you should be doing in the near future to accomplish the medium-range goals. Immediate goals are things you should be working toward right now to take you toward your short-term goals.

You can set daily, weekly and monthly goals to carry you toward your broader goals. The shorter the time-period involved, the more specific should be the goals. Put a date beside each one and make a determination to reach the goal by the specified date. Make the deadlines reasonable, but set goals that will stretch you.

Suppose your vision is to open your own business within 10 years, but your bank account at present is running on empty. Don't start your planning with the empty bank account. Start with the new business. What assets and qualifications will you need to open the business 10 years hence? Where will you need to be nine years from now — the year before the opening? To reach the nine-year milestone, where will you need to be five years from now? Where should you be two years from now to reach your five-year goal? A year from now to reach your two-year goal? Six months from now to reach your 12-month goal? What do you need to do *immediately* to meet your six-month goal?

Write these goals down and review them daily. They will help you keep your long-range commitment in mind and will keep you focused on the short-term steps you need to be taking to achieve your long-range goals.

SPECIFIC, MEASURABLE GOALS

A goal won't be effective if you don't make it specific and measurable. If your goal is to "lose weight" how will you know when you've fulfilled it? When you've lost a pound? When you've lost 10 pounds? With such a goal, you'll end up a year from now with the same figure or physique — and maybe a little more.

Set a specific goal and a specific date: "By July 1, I will have lost 15 pounds."

That gives you a specific target to shoot for by a specific date. And it's measurable. You can set intermediate goals to take you toward that objective: 10 pounds lost by June 1, five pounds by May 1, and three pounds by April 15.

Be similarly specific in your career goals: "By the time I'm 45 I will be earning $80,000 a year." Then you can set your medium-range goals: $65,000 by age 40, $55,000 by age 35, $40,000 by age 30, $35,000 by age 25.

INCLUDE EVERY ASPECT OF LIFE

Your vision should encompass every aspect of your life, because your future involves every aspect of your life. Therefore, you will need to set goals in different areas of life.

Your vision should take into account your physical, your mental and your emotional health. It should take into account your social, civic and spiritual lives.

Do you need to lose weight to achieve maximum health? Do you need to get your cholesterol level and your blood pressure down? Set goals in these areas and work with your doctor in achieving them.

Do you need to reduce stress levels to maintain proper mental and emotional balance? Do you need to become more active in service organizations? Are you devoting the proper amount of time to religious activities? Are you spending the proper amount of quality time with your family?

You can set specific, measurable goals in each of these areas.

ORGANIZATIONAL AND FAMILY GOALS

If you are part of an organization, chances are it has its own organizational vision. If you plan to become successful within that organization, you need to be familiar with its mission and goals. Your personal vision should support the organizational vision. Your personal goals should be developed in harmony with the organization's goals.

Family goals also need to be set in cooperation with other family members. You and your spouse should be clear on your visions and goals. If your vision calls for a larger home, do both of you share the vision? If so, you'll need to set goals for accumulating the financial resources to buy the home. Do you envision a place in the country while your spouse longs for a home in the upscale suburbs? You'll need to discuss the differences in your visions and work toward setting common goals.

USING YOUR RIGHT BRAIN

Goal-setting is a left-brain activity — a matter of judging and organizing. But your right brain can play a role in helping you meet your goals.

Goals can provide you with emotional tugs that draw you toward the achievement of your objectives. You can draw energy from your goals by absorbing them into your subconscious mind.

The subconscious has a variety of ways of receiving information. It takes it in through the eyes, through the ears, and through the senses of touch, taste and smell. It also takes it in through self talk — when you consciously think in words, your subconscious absorbs the words from your conscious mind.

When you write down your goals, you are forced to think the words as you write, so your subconscious absorbs the goals as self talk. When you read the words, you take in information through the eyes. When you speak them aloud, your auditory senses reinforce the message. Some people commit their goals to audio tapes, and listen to them each morning while getting ready for the day.

TURNING GOALS INTO AFFIRMATIONS

Some also turn their goals into affirmations. Affirmations are positive statements that express your goals as if they were already attained. The use of the present tense seems to add more certainty to the fulfillment of the goal. The subconscious mind accepts the goal as accomplished fact, and guides your behavior accordingly. Thus "I feel more energetic because I have lost 10 pounds" is more convincing to the subconscious than "I plan to gain more energy by losing 10 pounds."

Similarly, saying "I am the regional sales manager" is more likely to get you the job than saying "I will be promoted to regional sales manager." If you state your goals in the affirmative and in the present tense, your subconscious will cause you to act in a way that is consistent with your goals.

ADVERTISE YOUR GOALS

Advertise your goals. Some people keep their goals to themselves. They reason that if they tell the world what they hope to achieve, the whole world will laugh when they fall on their faces.

That's not necessarily true. Your acquaintances fall into three basic categories:

- ♦ Those who will be cheering for you whether you win or lose.

- ♦ Those who will be pulling for you to fail.

- ♦ Those who don't care one way or the other.

When you advertise your goals, your supporters will cheer you on and provide you with extra incentive to succeed. You'll also work harder to keep from embarrassing yourself in front of those who are pulling for you to fail. And you'll be motivated to sway the indifferent ones into your corner.

THE BENEFITS OF GOAL-SETTING

Goal-setting is the key to effective planning. It illuminates the road to success just as runway lights illuminate the landing field for an incoming aircraft.

Through goal-setting:

♦ You can direct your time, energy, talents, and skills into the areas where they will be most effective in taking you toward your vision.

♦ You can make the most effective use of your congenial competencies, using them to establish a meaningful pattern of success.

♦ You can identify the results you expect to achieve, measure your progress toward these results, and make mid-course corrections where necessary to assure the achievement of the results.

♦ You can identify the obstacles in the pathway of success and deal with them more effectively.

Just as you advertised your goals, advertise your success in reaching them. Advertise and celebrate. When you celebrate an achievement, you boost your morale and acquire the emotional energy to move on to the next goal. You also advertise your success and let the world know what you're capable of. You thus gain market value for yourself. As the anonymous wit wrote:

> *The codfish lays ten thousand eggs,*
> *The homely hen lays one.*
> *The codfish never cackles*
> *To tell you what she's done.*
> *And so we scorn the codfish*
> *While the humble hen we prize,*
> *Which only goes to show you*
> *That it pays to advertise.*

Each goal that you achieve takes you that much closer to your vision — that much closer to the future you desire. The achievement of that future means the achievement of success.

So set your goals, work to achieve them, advertise your success, and celebrate.

Chapter Nine

Set Priorities

---

*Wisdom ofttimes consists of knowing what
to do next.*

— Herbert Hoover.

Knowing what your goals are is one thing.
Knowing how to attain them is another.

To reach the goals you've set, you must learn to
direct your efforts in a systematic way in the direction
of your goals. This calls for setting priorities and planning your actions around the priorities.

PROACTIVE VS. REACTIVE APPROACHES

What should take priority in your daily life?

You can take either a reactive or a proactive approach. The reactive approach allows circumstances to set your priorities. The proactive approach allows you to set your own priorities.

In Chapter Four, you learned to perform situational triage to determine in what broad areas you would direct your energies.

You learned that effective people direct their efforts toward situations that they can influence, and that are worth influencing.

After you have identified the situations that are worth influencing, your next step is to establish your priorities in dealing with those situations.

IMPORTANT VS. URGENT

Your choices can be weighed by asking two basic questions:

♦ *What is most important?*

♦ *What is most urgent?*

Important choices are those that move you toward your goals. Urgent choices are choices that demand immediate attention.

The fewer *urgent* choices you have, the more time and energy you have to focus on the *important* choices.

Urgent choices come in the form of things that must be dealt with immediately to avoid undesirable consequences. They're best illustrated by the man who protested, "How can I concentrate on draining the swamp when I'm up to my waist in alligators?"

Many people spend so much time and energy fighting off individual alligators that they never get around to the main task, which is the draining of the swamp.

You encounter this dilemma in people who say, "I'd like to buy a new home, but I'm behind in my rent payments. If I don't catch them up I'll be evicted. That doesn't leave me any money to put aside for a down payment."

The rent payment is an urgent matter: If it isn't made, you won't have a place to live next month. But in the long run, more important than the month-by-month rent is the investment opportunity and long-term security to be enjoyed through home ownership.

How do you prevent the urgent from crowding out the important in your system of priorities?

One way is to plan ahead so that matters never reach the urgent stage.

THREE LEVELS OF PROBLEMS

Problems tend to move through stages, each with its own level of urgency. Level One is the proactive stage. At this point, the problem is just developing. You have plenty of time to deal with it, and only minor corrective action is needed to return things to normal.

If the problem is not addressed, it moves into Level Two — the reactive stage. At this point, some damage has probably been done, and it will have to be repaired before you can return things to normal. But the situation is not yet hopeless.

Level Two problems, left unattended, descend to Level Three — the crisis stage. At this point, you can no longer ignore the problem. Unless you do something immediately, the situation will become a disaster.

DRIFTING WITH THE CURRENT

To illustrate, imagine yourself fishing from a rowboat in a placid stream. You're aware that the current is slowly taking you downstream, but you know that you can drop an anchor at any time and stop the drifting. A few easy strokes of the oars will take you back to where you started. You are in the proactive stage at this point.

After allowing yourself to drift for a while, you become aware that the current is quickening. In the distance, you hear a faint murmur that tells you there's a waterfall ahead. You are now in the reactive phase. You can still drop anchor and stop the drift, but only with great difficulty will you be able to row back to your starting point. It may be necessary to row ashore and haul the boat overland. Intent on your fishing, though, you decide to drift a little further.

Soon, the murmur of the falls has become a deafening roar and the current has become a raging torrent. You can no longer propel your boat against it, and the anchor won't stop you. Ahead of you, the water surges over the falls. Unless you do something immediately, you will plunge over the falls, too — perhaps to your death. You are now at the crisis stage.

DRIFTING INTO FINANCIAL TROUBLE

Events in your life can follow this same pattern. You begin to make a few credit purchases that seem well within your budget. You know that you can pay them off in a few months and begin building up your savings again.

Then the economy dips and your income shrinks. Still, you're not strapped, and you buy a few more things on your credit card, just to maintain your standard of living.

Then you have some unexpected automobile repairs, and since you need your car to take you to work, you have to make them. You skip a rent payment to keep the car running. You're now in the reactive stage.

An unexpected illness puts you into the hospital, and you lose several weeks of work. You use up your sick leave, and the bills keep coming due. The landlord threatens to evict you, the bank threatens to repossess the car, and the boss says unless you're back on the job soon she'll be forced to replace you. You're entering the crisis stage.

AVOIDING THE CRISIS PHASE

Some people seem to live constantly in the crisis phase. Others seem to go through life avoiding the rough times. How do they do it?

By addressing problems while they're still in the proactive stage. This prevents unimportant things from turning into urgent situations that divert your time and attention away from important things.

Sometimes you have to clear the decks of urgent matters by accepting the undesirable consequences and moving on. If paying the rent on your present place is driving you to the financial brink, it may be necessary to move into less expensive accommodations until you have put your financial affairs in order. It may be necessary to drive a less expensive car, eat out less often and cut down on your entertainment budget.

These sacrifices require self-discipline, but you can muster the self-discipline if you have created a glowing vision and if you can see how the sacrifices help you to reach goals that lead toward the vision.

Successful people learn to pass up immediate pleasures in return for more gratifying long-term pleasures. They do the dull and unglamorous things that unsuccessful people are unwilling to do. By doing so, they avoid the recurring crises that result from neglecting things of long-term importance.

FOCUSING ON WHAT'S IMPORTANT

If you give priority to the important things and remain in the proactive mode, you'll find yourself giving increased attention to such things as relationship-building, new career opportunities, problem prevention, and family values.

Relationship-building is an important key to personal success. No one is truly a self-made person. Human society is built on cooperation, and we need to be able to count on the assistance of others.

Studies have shown an interesting difference between the behavior of high achievers and mediocre performers in the work place.

Both the star performers and the mediocrities look to others for assistance. But the star performers form networks before they need assistance. When the time comes to call for outside help, they know where to look.

Mediocrities, on the other hand, wait until they need help before looking around for assistance.

In other words, star performers look after the important things before they become urgent things.

HANDLING THE ROUTINE

All of us have to perform routine tasks that are not particularly important, but nevertheless must be done if we're to accomplish our work. We have to open mail, attend meetings, answer telephone calls, and deal with problems that others bring to our doorsteps.

Successful people learn to budget time for these chores, delegating routine tasks to other people when possible, and saving the bulk of their time for addressing the truly important issues.

DEVELOP A SYSTEM

Effective people also learn to ask: Is this necessary? Do you need to conduct a three-week study of a proposal when you already know most of what you need to know about it? If the study is nothing more than a formality, why not dispense with the formality and concentrate on things with higher priority? Do you need to compile a 50-page written report when the important information can be conveyed through a concise memo or a conversation over coffee?

You can relieve yourself of unimportant tasks by systematizing as much of your routine work as possible. For instance, if you have to write a lot of letters in response to inquiries, you can probably divide the inquiries into a few basic categories. Then, instead of having to compose a new letter for each individual inquiry, you could write a form letter for each category of inquiry. Stored on a computer disc, these letters could be called up and, with minor modification, used to answer nearly all of your inquiries.

END THE PAPER-SHUFFLING

A great deal of valuable time is wasted shuffling papers. I've worked out a system that gets me through this chore in short order and clears my desk for the truly important things.

When a letter comes across my desk, I read it and decide quickly whether I should handle it or refer it to someone else for action.

If it's something for someone else to handle, I write appropriate notes on the letter and immediately send it to the person who will handle it.

If it's something I need to handle, I take the appropriate action. I then respond to all the mail I plan to answer, filing as I go those letters I need to keep and discarding those I have no reason to keep.

When I've finished, I'm ready to tackle the important work.

The important work consists of the things you need to do to move you toward your goal. You establish your priorities by asking, "What needs to be done next if I am to move closer to my goal?

List the things that must take place before you reach your goal. Arrange them in the order that they need to occur.

When you've done this, you're ready to develop strategies for achieving your goals.

161

Chapter Ten

Develop Strategies

There usually are half a dozen right answers to "What needs to be done?" Yet unless a [person] makes the risky and controversial choice of only one, he will achieve nothing.

— Peter F. Drucker

Now that you have a vision, you have a set of goals leading to your vision, and you have determined what areas have priority in pursuing your goals, you need a set of strategies to take you to your goals.

Your strategies should meet these criteria:

♦ They must specify actions to be taken.

163

- They must specify the person or persons who is to take the actions.

- They must establish a time for beginning the actions.

- They must establish a deadline for completing the actions.

- They must establish criteria for determining when the actions have been satisfactorily completed.

WHAT HAS TO HAPPEN?

How do you decide what actions to take?

First, look at the goal you have set for yourself and ask, "What has to happen if I am to reach this goal?" Put your logical left brain to work and make a list of the things that must happen.

This may require some research on your part. If your goal is to open your own business, you'll need to answer questions such as:

- How much capital will I need to get started?

- Will I need to employ a staff, and if so, how many?

- What legal requirements must be met?

- What is the potential market for my products and services?

You may find answers in your public library or at your local Chamber of Commerce. You may have to consult a lawyer and accountant. It's wise to consult someone who has succeeded at a similar undertaking to learn what opportunities and pitfalls are out there.

MAKE A LIST

Acquire as much information as possible, then make a list of the things that must happen if you are to open your own business. Your list might include:

(1) Acquiring the necessary capital.
(2) Finding a suitable location.
(3) Recruiting qualified staff.
(4) Acquiring a starting inventory.
(5) Developing a marketing plan.
(6) Planning the grand opening.
(7) Advertising and promoting the opening events.

Now go down the list of things that must happen and ask, "How can I make it happen?" You have now posed a problem, which can be solved through a simple problem-solving process.

STATE THE PROBLEM

You begin moving toward the answer to your question by stating the problem:

"I need $200,000 in capital in order to start my business."

Now look for alternative ways of stating the problem:

"I need to obtain a delivery truck, a small warehouse, a showroom, and some office equipment and furniture."

You may be able to pick up a good used delivery truck and some surplus office furniture and equipment at bargain prices. Leasing instead of buying the office and warehouse space may reduce the amount of start-up capital you'll need.

Another way of stating the problem: "I need to find a way to expose my merchandise to potential customers and to deliver it to them."

The answer could be to use your garage or basement as warehouse space, using color brochures to introduce the merchandise to prospects, and letting your family van double as a delivery vehicle until you have grown your business.

LIST ALTERNATIVE APPROACHES

Restating the problem in this way can suggest alternative approaches. After you've stated the problem to your satisfaction, your next step is to list as many alternative approaches as you can. Here is where you may want to go into the creative right side of your brain. Let your mind wander over the possibilities. They might include:

♦ Cashing in or borrowing against your insurance policies.

♦ Going into your savings.

- Borrowing against the equity in your home.

- Borrowing from parents or in-laws.

- Borrowing from the Small Business Administration.

- Going into partnership.

- Taking on silent partners.

- Incorporating and selling stock.

At this stage, don't worry about the practicality of what you're proposing. Just get as many alternatives on paper as possible. If a few far-out ideas occur to you, write them down too. You never know when a crazy idea might provide the seed for a more rational and workable idea.

BRAINSTORM FOR IDEAS

You don't have to tackle the problem alone. Ask your family, friends and associates to help you brainstorm. Brainstorming can be a highly productive way of developing creative ideas.

The ground rules for brainstorming should be: "Anything goes." No suggestion should be too far out to land on the table. Ridicule should be banned so that everyone feels free to submit ideas without being considered ridiculous.

At this stage of problem-solving, you're relying solely on the creative right brain. The logical left brain should come into play only when it's time to decide which alternative is best.

BUILD AND COMBINE

Members of the brainstorming group should look for ways to build upon and combine the suggestions of others.

The best suggestions are those that can be visualized. Then it's possible to let the imagination play around with the suggestion.

One way to initiate creative thinking is to list all the assumptions made about an idea or an object. Take the simple case of a ball. What assumptions do we make about balls?

♦ Balls are round.

♦ Balls are thrown.

♦ When balls strike the ground, they usually bounce in the direction in which they have been thrown.

But suppose we change one or two of those assumptions:

♦ Balls are oval, not round.

♦ Balls may be kicked as well as thrown.

How does this affect other assumptions? If the oval ball lands on a pointed side, it may bounce in an unpredictable direction — even the direction opposite the one in which it was thrown or kicked. Now we have the makings of a great American sport. By changing two basic assumptions, we have sown the seeds for the New Year's bowl games and, ultimately, the Super Bowl.

USE A STORY BOARD

Another way of triggering creativity is through use of a story board. The method was pioneered by Walt Disney. You can use a blackboard or a bulletin board. Start by writing or posting a description of a problem you need to solve or a challenge you need to confront. Now let your family, friends and associates post their suggestions for ways to solve the problem or meet the challenge. Each person can post a suggestion that builds upon the previous suggestion.

SUMMON YOUR LEFT BRAIN

Whether you're brainstorming, using a story board, or following some other creative problem-solving process, you eventually reach the point at which it's time to summon your logical left brain. It's job is to evaluate the alternative solutions and narrow them down to the workable ones.

At first, the left brain should apply dynamic judgments. In making a dynamic judgment, you don't ask "Will this work?" Instead, you ask "How might we make this work?"

Certain responses should be ruled out from the beginning. They include:

- ◆ It's never been done before.

- ◆ It's too far-out to be considered.

- ◆ Our customers (or employees) are not ready for that.
- ◆ It's against company policy.

- ◆ That's not the way things are done around here.

After carefully examining the proposed alternatives, ask these questions about each:

- ◆ Is it implementable?

- ◆ Is it cost-effective (in terms of time, effort and emotional expense as well as dollars)?

- ◆ Does it move me toward my goal?

LIST ALTERNATIVES AND ACTION STEPS

Arrange the alternatives in the order of their effectiveness in taking you toward your goal. Then list the specific actions that must be taken to implement the solution.

If the action involves others besides yourself, designate the individual responsible for each action and set a starting date and a deadline for completing the action. Make clear the criteria you will use in deciding when an action has been completed. If the action involves finding a suitable location, the criterion might be the securing of an oral commitment, the signing of a lease, or the completion of any steps needed to enable you to move in.

In this chapter we've used the example of a person whose goal is to start a new business. But the same procedure can be followed to attain any goal. Just follow these steps:

(1) Decide what has to happen if your goal is to be attained.

(2) Ask what you need to do to make it happen, posing the question as a problem to be solved.

(3) Restate the problem to gain perspective.

(4) Make a list of alternative actions, using creative techniques such as brainstorming and story boarding.

(5) Use dynamic judgments to ask of each proposed action, "How can I make it work?"

(6) Compare the proposed actions and rank them according to their effectiveness is taking you toward your goal.

(7) Chose the most effective action course.

(8) Assign responsibility for each individual action, setting a starting date, a deadline for completion, and the criteria for determining when the action is completed.

When you have completed these steps, you will be ready for Step Four on your stairway to success: Preparation to act.

Creating an Action Plan

GOAL:	ACTION STEP	PERSON IN CHARGE	DATE TO BEGIN	DATE TO COMPLETE	HOW WELL KNOW

Figure 10-1

173

Stairway To Success

Prelude to Step Four

Ready, Set, Go!

For all your days, prepare,
And meet them ever alike;
When you are the anvil, bear;
When you are the hammer, strike.

—Edwin Markham

A good plan takes you nowhere. It only tells you where you expect to go. Tracing your route on a road map doesn't get you from Topeka to Los Angeles. Getting there requires that you hit the road.

But before you hit the road, there are preparations to make. You have to pack your bags, make sure your vehicle is in good condition, fill your gas tank and stock up on travelers' checks.

Action usually comes at the end of a series of preparatory steps, best described in the starter's words at the beginning of a race: *Get ready; Get set; GO!*

At the *Get ready* signal, foot racers assume a balanced stance that allows them to respond quickly when the action signal is given. Successful people acquire balance, too, in the physical, mental/ emotional, social and spiritual aspects of their lives.

When you achieve this state of equilibrium, you're ready to accept any challenge and conquer any barrier between you and success.

To acquire balance means to achieve that happy medium between minimum and maximum that represents your *optimum*. The minimum is the *least* you can get by with. The maximum is the *most* you're capable of. The optimum is the amount or degree of anything that is *most favorable toward the ends you desire.*

Let me illustrate the difference between *maximum* and *optimum*.

Your automobile may be capable of a maximum speed of more than 100 miles per hour, but if the end you desire is reliable, safe and comfortable transportation, you'll never drive it at top speed. At 100 miles per hour, you're subjecting it to excessive wear and the likelihood of a fatal crash.

At the other extreme, your car can crawl along at 5 to 10 miles per hour, minimizing the chances of your losing control on a curve, or crashing head-on into an object or rear-ending the vehicle ahead. But at such speeds your car is an inefficient form of transportation. It's wasting time and horsepower, and if other traffic is traveling at normal freeway speeds, it poses safety hazards.

Your car's optimum speed is a steady pace somewhere between those high and low speeds — probably between 55 and 65 miles per hour on an Interstate highway. That speed range usually provides the best combination of safety, fuel mileage, engine wear and travel time.

To use a human illustration, if you're running the marathon and you go all-out for the first mile, you may take an early lead, but the victory will go to the runner who strikes the highest *sustainable* pace. If the pace is too slow, the others will pass you. If it's too fast, you'll run out of energy before you reach the end of the race. You have to choose a happy medium.

You need to strike the same kind of balance in your personal habits and behavior.

Getting set entails bringing yourself to a motivational edge that allows you to put your heart and soul into the effort once the action has begun. Acquiring motivation means developing a strong reason to carry your action plan to a successful conclusion.

When you're balanced and motivated, you're ready to respond to the signal: *GO!*

Chapter Eleven

Get Ready Physically

Health and intellect are the two blessings of life.

— **Menander (c 342-292 b.c.)**

No matter what task you undertake, you'll do a better job if you feel good physically. You will tackle it with greater physical energy, more emotional vigor and greater intellectual sharpness.

That doesn't mean that only superb physical specimens in peak physical shape can expect to succeed in life. Stephen Hawkin, the noted British physicist, achieved scientific success although he suffered from a severely debilitating physical disease. Franklin Roosevelt led the nation through two of its worst

181

crises although he was permanently crippled by polio. Robert Louis Stevenson produced a body of literary classics while suffering from tuberculosis.

You may face health challenges that are outside your area of effective influence, but you can achieve optimum fitness within the limitations of your basic condition.

Generally speaking, physical fitness will result from seeking optimum balance in:

- ◆ Dietary habits.

- ◆ Exercise and rest.

- ◆ Work and relaxation.

- ◆ Sleep habits.

- ◆ Personal practices.

BALANCE IN EATING HABITS

Americans are well-fed and poorly nourished. Starvation is extremely rare in this country, but so is good nutrition. We eat plenty of the wrong kinds of foods. Therefore, we suffer from obesity, high cholesterol levels and other conditions that are directly related to diet.

The Wall Street Journal once referred to the American consumer's "workout, pig-out mentality." We engage in healthy exercise, then turn around and pig out on unhealthy food.

Sometimes a poor diet is the result of imbalance in other areas of life. Many people use food as an antidote for depression, but it seldom works. The self-indulgent resort to chocolate, pizza, beer and chips results in more weight gain, which in turn feeds the depression.

At the other extreme are people who starve themselves out of fear of becoming too fat. Each of us has an optimum weight, which depends largely upon our age, our sex, and our height. Your doctor can quickly tell you your optimum weight and recommend a regimen for attaining it.

A balanced, nutritional diet will help you maintain optimum mental and physical alertness. It will help you to maintain your optimum weight, which not only helps you feel more energetic, but also increases your self-confidence and helps you to make a good impression on others. When you feel good, look good and feel confident, you have a head start on success in whatever you undertake.

BALANCE IN PHYSICAL EXERCISE

Maintaining your optimum weight requires more than proper eating. It also requires regular exercise. The formula isn't complicated. You eat food to provide fuel for your body's activities. When you eat more food than your body burns, the fuel is stored away as fat, and you gain weight. When you eat less food than your body burns, the stored-up fat is consumed and you lose weight. Therefore, you can lose weight either by cutting down on your food intake or by increasing your physical activity.

I try to keep my weight close to the optimum level for my height, age and sex. But sometimes I yield to temptation and have an extra candy bar or junk-food snack between meals. When I do that, I atone with an extra helping of exercise — a jog around the block, or perhaps a few minutes on an exercise bike.

Exercise is important for reasons other than controlling weight. It is vital for keeping your muscles in optimum condition. The best way to keep them in shape is to use them regularly. The most important muscle of all is your heart. Physical exercise causes it to pump more rapidly, thus building up its strength.

Sedentary lifestyles are among the most common causes of cardio-vascular diseases. Yet some studies have indicated that fewer than 40% of us engage in sports or other forms of physical activity for as much as one hour a week.

Not only can regular exercise be fun; it also makes you feel good. And when you're feeling good, you're bound to do a better job.

As a speaker and a consultant, I know that I'm going to be at my best when I'm in optimum physical condition. When I'm feeling good, it puts the sharp edge on my presentations, whether I'm keynoting a sales convention or counseling a top-management team. When I'm physically down, I can sometimes force myself to rise to the occasion, but I wouldn't be able to do that consistently, week in and week out. Physical fitness is something you can't fake for long.

Exercise is the key to fitness, and it doesn't have to be a chore. A brisk 20-minute stroll in the early morning or during your lunch break can be a pleasant but significant contribution to your physical health. So can bicycle riding. Jogging, tennis, badminton, handball, volleyball and other physical activities can be fun and healthy at the same time.

But remember the principle of balance: The quest for physical fitness can be carried to the extreme. When physical fitness becomes the central focus of your life; when exercise becomes an end in itself rather than a means toward an end, you're out of balance.

BALANCE IN WORK AND RELAXATION

One of the principles you learned from the cradle onward is that "all work and no play makes Jack a dull boy." It also makes Jill a dull girl.

The converse is also true: All play and no work makes Jill and Jack dull persons. Balance between work and play is an important factor in your physical well-being.

The consequences of all play and no work are well known. Aesop dramatized them in his fable of the ant and the grasshopper. The grasshopper frolicked all summer and ended up with nothing to sustain it during the winter. The ant used the summer months to store up provisions.

People who spend all their time having a ball often have nothing to go home to after the ball is over. Life can't be one continuous party. If you expect to achieve true happiness, you have to build a solid foundation for success. That means learning new things and applying the things you learn.

If you're pursuing success in a congenial role in a compatible career, you should find learning to be stimulating and even fun. Applying the things you learn should give you great satisfaction, because it means you're getting better and better at the things you enjoy doing.

Does that mean that all your waking hours should be spent on the job, or going to seminars and night classes?

Of course not. The occasional night on the town, the week-end vacation and even a pressure-free day of goofing off (as long as you're not goofing off on somebody else's time) can be refreshing and beneficial. But if partying and goofing off are your normal routine, you need to look for balance. The secret of balance is knowing when to be the ant and when to be the grasshopper.

We have a name for people who never allow themselves to step out of the ant role. We call them workaholics. Workaholics believe they can achieve success by working round the clock. This would be true if our minds and bodies were capable of sustaining high-quality performance indefinitely. But they're not. Just as a race car needs to make a pit stop at certain intervals for maintenance and repair, so your body needs regular rest to keep its components in good functioning order.

In most pursuits, success is not just measured by quantity. Quality is usually even more important, and this applies whether you're laying bricks or crunching numbers. Brick-layers who work 16-hour days will not produce the same quality at 11 p.m. as they did at 11 a.m., especially if they repeat the routine day in and day out. Physical and mental fatigue take their toll. Accountants who bury their heads in figures in round-the-clock efforts to complete their audits will find mistakes starting to crop up as the evening wanes. Writers and artists will find their creativity dulling as fatigue sets in.

When people love their work, they're often willing to put in more than the standard eight-hour day. One characteristic of high achievers is that they tend to show up earlier and stay later than their colleagues. But when work consistently consumes your waking hours to the near-total exclusion of recreational activities, you are courting physical and mental burnout.

I'm a hard worker. I love what I do, and I spend a lot of time at it. I often drop by my office late at night, or go in for a couple of hours early in the morning. But I also make time for my family and for recreational activities. Since much of my work involves the creation and execution of ideas, I keep a notepad handy, even when I'm relaxing on the beach. But I do relax. I could not provide my clients and my business associates with my best efforts if I didn't find some time to recharge my batteries. More important, I could not live up to my principles as a devoted family man if I didn't spend time relaxing and enjoying the company of my wife and children.

It may be necessary at times to work long hours to accomplish a specific purpose or to deal with a specific situation. If you're in college and you have to work to support yourself, you may find yourself sacrificing playtime for study and work time. But you can do this knowing that when your goal is achieved and you have a degree in hand, you can pursue a more balanced schedule.

In your work life, you may face deadlines or encounter emergencies that require you to work longer than your normal hours, and successful people are willing to do this. But if these situations become the rule rather than the exception, you need to examine your work habits or even your line of work. Neither a race car nor a human can go flat-out indefinitely without experiencing a breakdown.

Give yourself a break. Regularly. If you don't, you'll find your inventory of stress building up, and with stress comes physical problems. It breeds headaches, stomach problems, fatigue, muscular tension and nervous irritability. It can be the underlying cause of cancer and cardio-vascular ailments. It is a major enemy of optimum performance.

BALANCE IN SLEEP

Your body needs sleep. Some of us seem to be able to get by with less sleep than others can. But for most adults, seven to eight hours of sleep per night is optimum.

In most cases, your body can tell you when you're getting enough sleep. If you need an alarm clock to awaken you at the proper time in the morning, you're probably staying up too late.

When you short-change yourself on sleep, your body short-changes you on performance. You can't give your optimum effort when you're drowsy and nodding. Nor can you start your day in top form when you sleep until the last minute, throw some cold water on your face and rush through your dressing routine. Not only will you not perform at your best; you'll not look your best either.

Getting the proper amount of sleep is usually a matter of scheduling. If your day starts early in the morning, don't allow yourself to get hooked on the late-night television shows — unless entertainment is at the core of your value systems and making a living is near the bottom of your priorities.

If you take work home with you, try to put it aside and do something relaxing an hour or two before retiring. Light reading or relaxing music can pave the way to pleasant dreams.

Don't drink coffee, tea or any other stimulant during the hours approaching bedtime. Midnight snacks can also keep you awake. An alcoholic night-cap may help you relax, but a second drink can keep you awake, and repeated drinks will reward you with a hangover in the morning.

If you still have trouble going to sleep at a reasonable hour, you may find it helpful to use relaxation techniques. A number of audiotapes are available to put you into a soothing, relaxed mood.

You can also relax on your own by getting comfortable, closing your eyes, breathing deeply and rhythmically, and letting your imagination transport you into a quiet, beautiful, tension-free setting, such as a seashore or a mountain retreat. Visualize your surroundings as if you were actually there, letting yourself feel the wind on your skin, hear the sound of crashing waves or rippling current, and smell the fragrance of the outdoors.

Usually, if you make it a habit to retire at a reasonable hour and arise at a reasonable hour, you'll find that sleep comes naturally and pleasantly.

If none of this works for you, ask your doctor to recommend a way to get the proper amount of sleep.

Sometimes we wake up naturally after the proper amount of sleep, then turn over for one last snooze before getting up. Make it a practice to get out of bed as soon as you awake.

This may take a little effort at first, but in time it will become a habit.

Get up in time to eat a nutritious breakfast. Try to have breakfast *with* someone — a spouse, a friend, a client or a colleague. A pleasant, stimulating conversation over breakfast can be a good way to wake up your mental and physical faculties before you turn to your daily tasks.

BALANCE IN PERSONAL HABITS

You don't have to give up all the physical pleasures to lead a healthy lifestyle. You don't have to eliminate meat from your diet, pass up desserts, and drink nothing but fruit juice and water.

But you do have to understand that many things that bring pleasure have expensive price tags attached. Only you can decide whether the pleasure is worth the price. Some pleasures are virtually harmless when pursued in moderation. Others are dangerous at any level.

Whether to use tobacco is one of those decisions that individuals must make for themselves. Inhaling tobacco smoke entails risks, and the more you inhale the greater the risk.

Dr. Louis Sullivan, Secretary of Health and Human Services under President Bush, claimed that the yearly death toll from tobacco in the United States exceeds the death toll from all four years of American participation in World War II. Tobacco has been blamed for 90% of all lung cancer in males over 45 years old.

Athletic coaches recognize that smoking inhibits physical performance by cutting down on the efficiency of the lungs.

These facts have been widely publicized. But many people may be unfamiliar with other consequences of heavy smoking.

For instance, studies have shown that absenteeism from the job is 40% higher among smokers than among non-smokers. A study by the state of Maine showed that cigarette smokers missed more time from work because of back problems than did non-smokers. Those who suffered injuries on the job were more likely to be smokers than those who were not injured. And the injured smokers, on average, smoked more cigarettes than did the uninjured smokers.

So smoking tobacco — particularly heavy smoking — can hamper physical performance and even result in physical disability.

In view of the current trend toward ever tighter restrictions on smoking in public, it's also wise to consider the consequences of working while experiencing an unsatisfied craving for a smoke. You can't very well concentrate your mental or physical energies on the task at hand while your mind and body are crying for a cigarette break.

Alcohol is another popular source of pleasure and trouble.

Used in moderation, alcohol can be pleasant and relaxing, and some say it may actually reduce the chances of heart trouble. But alcohol abuse is one of the more widespread problems in our society. It has been blamed for a third of the traffic injuries in the United States and for nearly three out of five traffic fatalities. It is involved in a third of the suicides, two out of five fatal industrial accidents, and seven out of 10 fatalities resulting from drowning, fires and falls.

While alcohol, in moderation, may make you more relaxed during social encounters, remember that it is a depressant. Neither your mental nor your physical capacities are at their optimum when you're under the influence of alcohol. Alcohol is the enemy in tasks that require mental concentration or physical coordination.

Furthermore, alcohol tends to remove unconscious inhibitions. That's why the shy introvert often relaxes and becomes more sociable after a drink. But inhibitions are control mechanisms, and when they begin to fall you begin to lose that control. In delicate negotiations or any situation that requires a calm, cool control of your reactions, leave alcohol out of the equation.

Mind-altering drugs pose another threat to success. Some people think drugs can enhance creativity and increase your chances of success. But there are techniques for enhancing creativity without assaulting your brain with chemicals.

Even if it were true that mind-altering drugs are the gateway to creativity leading to success, you'd have to ask: success by what definition? Too often, the drugs that accompany creative success drive the user to emotional disaster. The person whose lifetime of success is cut short by an accidental overdose or deliberate suicide is not a successful person at all.

Statistics indicate that mind-altering drugs do not promote on-the-job excellence. Quite the contrary. Herman Miller, a Michigan furniture manufacturer, instituted a policy of drug testing for new employees. It found that those who tested positive for marijuana had medical claims 10 times as high as those who tested negative. Marijuana users took 50% more personal time away from their jobs than non-users did, and usually quit their jobs or were discharged more quickly.

Balanced individuals recognize that neither drugs nor alcohol are tools for success. They are more likely to lead to disaster, either through accidents or through the deterioration of body and mind.

Regardless of what people tell you, you cannot function at optimum physical and mental efficiency while under the influence of alcohol and drugs.

MAKE PHYSICAL FITNESS A PLEASURE

Physical fitness is a pleasant way to prepare yourself for success. With a little imagination and experimentation, you can find delicious foods that are also healthy and nutritious. You can choose from a variety of activities that provide fun along with healthy exercise. You will learn the pleasures of rest and relaxation in preparing you for the exertions required to succeed. You will find that balancing work and recreation keeps you alert and sharp. You will discover in a life without drugs and addictive habits a new freedom to control your thoughts, your feelings — and your destiny.

Acquire physical balance. And then move on to achieve balance in your mental, spiritual, and emotional life.

Chapter Twelve

Get Ready Mentally and Emotionally

The mind is its own place, and in itself can make heaven of Hell, a hell of Heaven.

— John Milton

Rudyard Kipling, the British writer, once penned a poem of basic advice for young people. In it, he maintained that the world and everything that's in it is yours:

> *If you can talk with crowds and keep your*
> *   virtue,*
> *Or walk with kings — nor lose the common*
> *   touch,*
> *If neither foe nor loving friend can hurt you,*
> *And all men count with you, but none too*
> *   much.*

Kipling was describing mental and emotional balance. To succeed, you must be able to deal with people of all sorts, listening to their ideas and observing their values without compromising your own principles. You must deal confidently with those above you in the chain of authority, while maintaining open communication with those below you. You must be secure enough in who you are to take criticism from friend and foe. When someone you love disappoints you, you can't let the disappointment destroy you. You must respect the values and opinions of others without allowing others to control your life.

You can achieve this mental and emotional balance by following these steps:

1. Recognize your own self-worth.
2. Destroy the Gloom Bug.
3. Acquire perspective.
4. Be patient.
5. Acquire a sense of humor.
6. Learn to deal with conflict.
7. Cultivate successful expectations.

RECOGNIZE YOUR OWN SELF-WORTH

One of the greatest mistakes you can make is to underestimate yourself. It's far worse to under-estimate than it is to overestimate.

The reason is quite simple: You act in harmony with the way you see yourself. If you overestimate your ability to accomplish something, you will act as if you can do it. And usually, by stretching your abilities to the limit, you can accomplish what you set out to do.

But if you underestimate your ability, you will either pass up the challenge, or you will tackle the job only half-heartedly.

There are some who say that the bumblebee greatly overestimates her ability to fly. Her body is much too large for the flimsy set of wings nature gave her. But the bumblebee *thinks* she can fly, she flaps her wings as if she *expects* to fly, and guess what: She *flies*, and she flies very well.

Americans are taught from grade school on that all people are created equal. But many of us take that to be just a high-sounding phrase. It's more than a phrase; it's true. Nobody on earth is more valuable than you are. Your life is as precious to you as the greatest people's lives have been to them. And *your* estimate of your self-worth is the only estimate that counts. What other people think about you is your *reputation*. What you think about yourself represents your *true worth*. Thomas Edison's teachers thought he was just another hard-of-hearing, slow-witted kid. Edison knew better, and he showed them.

You are a bundle of potential. All you need to do is to convince yourself that the potential is there. How do you convince yourself?

You *tell* yourself.

You talk to yourself throughout your waking hours. Your lips may not be moving, but your brain is sending out a constant stream of thoughts, and these thoughts are framed in words.

When you spill sauce on your best clothes, you think, "Oh my, look what I've done! And I just got this outfit out of the cleaners!"

That's your conscious mind speaking. You also have an unconscious mind. It's the portion of your mind that stores all the memories that you call on when you need them. You don't go around all day thinking about April 15. Yet that date is stored in your memory, along with the knowledge that it represents the deadline for filing your federal income-tax refund. You might say that you put them out of your mind until it's time to think about your taxes, but it's really not out of your mind. It's like data stored on a computer disk. The data may not be visible on the screen, but they're there to be called up when needed. Your unconscious mind is comparable to a computer disk. Your conscious mind is comparable to a computer's monitor screen. The unconscious mind holds much more information than the conscious mind can keep track of all at once.

The important thing to remember is that *the unconscious mind believes what the conscious mind tells it*. When a conscious thought flits through your mind, your unconscious mind "hears" it, believes it, and records it. Your conscious mind may forget about it immediately, but it's on permanent file in your unconscious.

Your unconscious mind is the storehouse for your habits—all the things you do without consciously thinking about them.

200

Therefore, your unconscious mind has a profound effect on the way you act.

When your unconscious mind hears you think "I'm clumsy," it believes you and it moves you to act clumsily. If it hears you say "I'll never learn the Texas two-step," it will believe you, and you won't learn the Texas two-step.

Pessimists are always feeding their unconscious minds with negative thoughts. Their unconscious minds believe what they hear, and the pessimism becomes self-fulfilling prophecy.

The team that goes into a contest expecting to lose will lose. The team that confronts a superior team with the confidence that it can score an upset is quite likely to pull off an upset.

Therefore, it's important that you make a conscious decision: *I will allow myself to think only positive thoughts about myself.*

You may say, "How can I think positive thoughts all the time? Nothing good ever happens to me."

That's the first negative thought you need to banish from your mind.

Your experiences are like coins. Each has a heads and a tails. Successful people learn to flip their coins to the other side.

For instance, if you've been planning for a week-end of golf and the weather suddenly turns wet and blustery, you might say, "What a bummer! My week-end is ruined." Or you might flip to the other side of the coin: "Well, no golf this week-end. But what an opportunity to improve my bowling game!"

If you made an error on the job that cost the company money, you might say, "What a goof-off I am! One more blunder like that and I'd better look for another job."

Or you might flip the coin over and say: "Now that I know what I did wrong, I'll never make that mistake again. That clears away one more obstacle to success."

When you do something well, congratulate yourself. Tell yourself how good you are. Don't be humble; you deserve the praise! When you fail to meet your usual standards, tell yourself that this isn't typical of you. You can do better. And do it!

Respect those who have accomplished great things in life, but don't be intimidated by them.

Once there was a farmer who became interested in politics and eventually was elected governor of his state. As a governor, he had an opportunity to meet some of the greatest leaders of his day: senators, ambassadors, Cabinet members, elder statesmen, former presidents, presidential candidates, and even the president himself.

The farmer told himself: "These people are no greater than I am. I can accomplish anything they can accomplish."

So he decided to try for the White House. And Jimmy Carter became our 39th president.

If people tend to underestimate you, don't be discouraged. Tell yourself: "They don't know me the way I know myself. I'll show 'em." Then go out and show them!

If you try and don't succeed, find out why you didn't succeed, then look for ways to eliminate the cause of the failure. When you do that, you're turning a pattern of failure into a stairway toward success.

Remember: You're never a failure. You're just a success waiting to happen. When you start thinking of yourself in this way, you will succeed.

DESTROY THE GLOOM BUG

When you acquire mental and emotional balance, you hold yourself accountable for your own success, accept responsibility for your own failures, and take the initiative in turning setbacks into lessons in success.

Successful people learn from others, accept advice and counsel from others, and welcome the assistance of others. But they don't put others in charge of their lives, and they don't blame others when things go wrong. Following Kipling's advice, all people count with them, "but none too much." They look at life proactively, controlling events instead of letting events control them; listening to advice from others, but making up their own minds about whether to follow it.

People who put other people in charge of their lives or entrust their destiny to the flow of events are vulnerable to depression — a disease spread by the GLOOM BUG.

Depression often results when people disappoint you or the tide of fate seems to be flowing against you, but you don't have to let these things depress you. Your problem is not what has happened or who caused it to happen; it's how you feel about what's happened.

So the cure for depression is to change the way you feel about things.

People can be depressed and not realize it. Here's how depression works:

- ◆ You constantly think in negative and illogical ways.

- ◆ As a result of your negative thinking, you have bad moods.

- ◆ Your bad moods bring on more pessimistic thoughts and actions, creating a vicious cycle.

When you're in depression, that low-grade virus has become a full-fledged bug. You have a few bad breaks and you let these breaks lead you into negative thought patterns.

Before you know it, you're stricken with the Gloom Bug. Here are some thought patterns that bring on the GLOOM BUG:

Grayless perceptions.

Leaping to conclusions.

Over-generalization.

Minimizing the positive.

Blaming yourself.

Unrealistic emotions.

Gotta do's.

When you're in the throes of *grayless perceptions*, you see everything in black or white. If you're not doing everything right, then you're doing everything wrong. If you're not a total success you're a total failure. There are no gray areas.

When you *leap to conclusions*, you assume that whatever happens is for the worst. You assume, without any evidence, that people are reacting negatively to you. You expect the worst, then accept your expectation as the reality.

You *over-generalize* by accepting a single set-back as a pattern of failure. If you make one goof, you tell yourself, "I'm a failure." If someone annoys you one time, you say to yourself, "That person is a jerk."

Overgeneralization will lead you to focus on a single negative detail and let it color your whole outlook. You make one mistake, you base your self-esteem on it, forgetting about all the right things you do over the long haul. It's like Michael Jordan basing his self-image on one baseball strike-out, without considering the brilliant record he compiled as a basketball superstar.

Sometimes we cheat ourselves of self-esteem by **minimizing the positive**, telling ourselves that upbeat experiences are insignificant. At the same time, we're willing to hold on to a negative belief that is contrary to everyday experience. We exaggerate the shortcomings of ourselves and others while minimizing strengths and assets.

Some people *blame themselves* for everything negative that happens, even when they had nothing to do with it. They believe that somebody has to be to blame for everything, and, noble souls that they are, they step in and accept it. Self-blame sends them on a guilt trip that compounds their depression.

Don't let *unrealistic emotions* take control. You assume that your emotions represent reality. You *feel* inadequate, so you must *be* inadequate. You *feel* like a failure, so you must *be* a failure.

Many people put their lives on auto-pilot, letting them be guided by an illogical assortment of things they've *"gotta do."*

They are always telling themselves, or others, that they've "gotta do" this or they "mustn't do" that. They live in a world of "should." When they don't do what they feel they should do, they feel guilty.

The GLOOM BUG can be controlled with a piece of flypaper and some *Reality Spray*.

First you trap the bug it on the flypaper, then you apply the reality spray.

The flypaper is a chart on which you write down the thoughts that are getting you down. Then you identify the type of negative thinking they represent. Next you state the reality that contradicts the negative thought.

Figure 12-1 is an example of the way an individual might use a piece of flypaper.

Figure 12-2 is a piece of flypaper you can use to identify any negative thoughts you might have.

Think of some negative thoughts you might have had about yourself. Enter them on the Flypaper. Identify the type of Gloom Bug they represent, and apply the reality spray.

ACQUIRE PERSPECTIVE

Up close, the earth looks flat. From outer space, it's round. The difference is in perspective.

On the ground, the Andes look impassable. From a jetliner flying at 40,000 feet, they shrink to manageable size. From the space shuttle, they're hardly noticeable. The difference is in perspective.

When we see things in perspective, we see them in their proper relationships as to value or importance. Different people have different perspectives. People in their 70s see time in a different perspective from those in their 20s. A multi-millionaire sees a $300,000 home in a different perspective from a salaried person earning $30,000 a year.

A person planning to drive to the next block may see the potholes in the street from a perspective quite different from one who plans to drive across the continent.

People often fail to look at their lives in perspective. They are so concerned with immediate things that they don't bother to take the long view. That's because they don't expect to go very far. The hourly worker looks ahead only to the end of the present shift. The supervisor charged with maintaining the employee's records may look ahead only to the end of the pay period. The manager may have to set annual goals, and thus work from a wider perspective. The CEO may have to think of market trends in 25-year cycles.

If you plan to go far in life, you have to adopt a long-range perspective.

What may be viewed as a major obstacle to the worker trying to get to the end of the shift may be just a temporary nuisance to the manager looking a year into the future. What may look like a major economic disruption to the manager with the 12-month view may be seen by the CEO as a mere blip in the long-term cycle.

Acquiring perspective enables you to respond realistically to the events in your life. The teen-ager whose sweetheart has just found another love may be distraught, convinced that romance has died forever. The parent, looking at it from the perspective of years, knows that the next "true love" is just a wink and a smile away.

The person without perspective will go through life making erratic decisions. Salespeople without perspective will make major changes in the presentation after each rejection, and thus never stick with an approach long enough to know whether it really works in the long run. Managers without perspective will keep their staffs in confusion, often taking emergency approaches to problems that will work themselves out, given time. Entrepreneurs will try one enterprise after another, interpreting each setback as a failure, never sticking with one effort long enough to achieve success.

BE PATIENT

Patience is the balance between boldness and prudence; between rashness and wisdom. It is illustrated in the fable of the golden goose. The goose produced a golden egg each day, but that wasn't enough for the impatient owner. He decided to slaughter the goose and harvest all the eggs at once. The result: no more goose and no more eggs.

Poet-philosopher Ralph Waldo Emerson gives sound advice: "Adopt the pace of nature: Her secret is patience."

Impatience is what causes people to give up on their goals before their efforts have had a chance to bear fruit. Patient people learn to distinguish between disasters and temporary setbacks. When things don't work out, they ask "Why?" Then they turn the "why" into "how" and begin developing strategies to convert the setback into a success.

When you develop your action plan, set realistic timetables. If the timetable you've set seems to be unrealistic, remember that most things take longer than you think they do. Recalculate, make your adjustments, and keep moving toward your goal. Remember Yogi Berra's famous dictum: "It ain't over till it's over."

ACQUIRE A SENSE OF HUMOR

Nothing softens the blows of life like a good sense of humor. How often have you had an experience that you considered humiliating, mortifying, and even degrading at the time but that you were later able to tell about with laughter?

If it's funny in retrospect, why wasn't it funny at the time?

The answer is in your *reaction* to it. If you can learn to look for the humor at the time of the experience, you'll save yourself a lot of emotional pain, and you'll cause other people to be more comfortable around you.

LEARN TO DEAL WITH CONFLICT

There's no such thing as a life without conflict. The history of humanity has been a history of conflicts. But not all conflict is destructive and not all conflict is bad.

You will encounter two basic types of conflict: personal and interpersonal.

Personal conflict arises when you are confronted with two or more conflicting options. The options may involve conflicting needs or desires. They may arise from conflicting values. You will encounter several types of personal conflict:

- ♦ *Positive/positive.* You may be planning to use your annual bonus to take a vacation in Europe, but you encounter an attractive investment opportunity, and you can't afford the investment and the vacation in the same year. You have a conflict between two positive actions and you have to decide which one to take.

♦ *Positive/negative.* You've been looking for a position in marine biology, a career choice that is in harmony with your congenial competencies. An opportunity comes along that offers good pay, good hours and great benefits. But it would require you to live in Alaska, and you hate cold weather. You have to decide whether the negative factors outweigh the positive.

♦ *Negative/negative.* You've submitted the low bid on a contract, and you immediately realize that you made a mistake. If you accept the job, you'll lose money. If you pass it up, the work will go to a competitor and you may lose the customer's long-term business. You have to decide between two negatives: losing money on the contract or losing the opportunity to obtain future business from the customer.

If you are focused on your vision and your goals and have an action plan in place, decisions involving personal conflict can be reached more easily. You simply choose the option that will move you closer to your goal in harmony with your action plan. Of course, your action plan should be subject to change to accommodate opportunities that will move you toward your goal more quickly and easily.

Interpersonal conflict occurs when people who live or work together have different values, goals and viewpoints. When the time comes to act, there is disagreement. One person's interests may conflict with another's. Anger and resentment often result.

Often, differences can be resolved by considering the other person's preferred behavioral mode. If you understand what motivates the other person, you may be able to reach a compromise that will satisfy the emotional needs of both parties. Give the Top-Gun an opportunity to win. Give the Engager a chance to look good. Satisfy the Accommodator's need to feel secure. And find a way to satisfy the meticulous person's need for logic and order.

This is the win/win approach to conflict resolution. When you take this approach, you look upon the conflict not as a battle that must be won, but as a problem that must be solved. The parties to the conflict get together and define the problem. Then they explore creative solutions.

EXPECT TO SUCCEED

Success rarely comes to those who are expecting failure. If you think you're going to fail, you're going to fail. If you expect to succeed, you're likely to succeed.

Studies have shown that people tend to live up to high expectations. Classroom experience has shown that children of ordinary ability whose teachers expect them to perform well will do better than more gifted children whose teachers hold low expectations for them.

The children adopt the teacher's expectations and perform accordingly.

If you hold high expectations for yourself, you will perform up to those expectations. If you hold low expectations, you will perform down to them.

That's why it's important to aim high with your vision and to set ambitious goals. If you expect above-average performance from yourself, you'll get it.

As you meet the ambitious goals you set for yourself, your confidence will grow, your expectations of success will be higher and you will move on to greater achievements.

One way to create the expectation of success is to visualize yourself doing something perfectly. This is called mental rehearsal. In one famous experiment, members of a basketball team were divided into three groups. One group practiced free throws in the gym for 20 minutes a day for a month. Another group stayed away from the gym, but each player spent 20 minutes a day visualizing himself making perfect free throws. The third group neither practiced nor visualized.

At the end of the month, the group that practiced in the gym had improved its free-throw average by 24%. The group that visualized itself making free throws improved by 23%. The third group showed no improvement.

The experiment provides dramatic evidence of the power of the subconscious mind. When the players consciously "saw" themselves making the perfect free throws, the subconscious was unable to distinguish between the visualization and reality. It therefore believed the players were successfully making the shots. When the time came actually to make the shots, the subconscious mind set up the expectation of success that led to improved free-throw shooting.

You can use this same technique in whatever you are undertaking. Visualize yourself executing the strategies in your action plan, moving steadily and surely toward your goals. Imagine how you will feel when you have successfully completed each step.

For example, if you're in sales, visualize yourself giving an effective sales presentation. In your imagination, allow the prospect to raise tough objections, and visualize yourself overcoming them, skillfully closing the sale. Imagine yourself receiving a plaque as salesperson of the year, winning a free trip to Hawaii, and enjoying the fruits of your success.

If your goal is to move into a management position, visualize yourself in your executive office suite. Imagine the way you would run your department, fashioning creative solutions to business challenges. See yourself enjoying the benefits of an executive's salary and enjoying the perks of management.

PUT YOURSELF IN CHARGE

People who enjoy mental and emotional balance are self-reliant and self-determining. They don't blame their troubles or shortcomings on any person, circumstance or system.

They look within themselves for answers as to how things got to be a certain way and how things can be changed for the better.

They know that if they don't accept responsibility for their own circumstances, nobody else will. They will graciously accept help, but they are far more concerned with giving it. They make their decisions based on their own values and judgments. They work toward their own goals and live up to their own standards, respecting the views of others but refusing to be controlled by them.

If Columbus had been overly concerned about the views of others, he would never have sailed Westward.

If Robert Fulton had been governed by others' perceptions, he would never have built a steamboat.

If the Wright brothers had been bound by others' perspectives, they would have remained earthbound.

Dream your own dreams and pursue your own goals. When you dream and act in harmony with your dream, you create a powerful current that can sweep you toward the realization of your dream.

Gloom-Killing Flypaper

Negative Thought	Type of Gloom Bug	Reality Spray
I'm a lousy manager. My best staff person just turned in her resignation.	Blaming yourself	Nonsense. We had a great relationship. She left to go back to school for an advanced degree.
I'm a failure at sales. My volume last month was down 5% compared with the previous month.	Grayless perceptions	So what. The previous month was my best in the past five years. Last month's volume was my fourth highest total, and I achieved it without resorting to the special discounts offered the previous month.

Figure 12-1

Gloom-Killing Flypaper

Negative Thought	Type of Gloom Bug	Reality Spray

Figure 12-2

218

Chapter Thirteen

Get Ready Socially

We are all dependent on one another, every soul of us on earth.

— George Bernard Shaw

Humans were not made to live and work alone. They were designed for the companionship of other humans. No individual ever built a civilization. Every society has been built upon the cooperative efforts of many individuals.

It follows, then, that individuals succeed by working with other individuals. You will be unable to execute your action plans alone. You will need the help of others, and you will have to build upon the foundations of many others.

American philosopher Abraham Maslow developed a pyramid to illustrate the basic human needs. At the base of that pyramid are the bare essentials for human existence: food, clothing and shelter, which he calls "physiological needs." These are the fundamental needs humans strive to meet.

Once we have satisfied these basic needs, we move up to the next level of the pyramid: safety needs. These represent the things we need to secure ourselves against threats to our existence.

Once we have achieved security, we begin working on the next level of human needs: the need to belong to a social group. The fourth level is the achievement of ego-satisfaction, or self-esteem. The final level is "self actualization" — becoming all that you can be.

Notice that social needs are near the foundation of the pyramid, just above food, clothing, and shelter, and the need for safety. You can satisfy them by focusing your attention on these areas:

- ♦ Your family.

- ♦ Your community.

- ♦ Your work place.

- ♦ Your leisure activities.

ACQUIRE SOCIAL BALANCE

To be socially balanced means to be a participating member of society. Society is made up of a wide variety of social units. The basic unit is the family, but beyond the family doorstep lie the schools, the community, governmental programs and agencies and all the organizations that hold the community together.

These social units provide you with important services, but they themselves need to be nourished by human efforts.

A person who is socially unbalanced takes from this menu of social services without giving anything in return. Such individuals remain perpetually dependent on society, but they exist only at the subsistence level. They're like the slave in the parable of Jesus, who took the talent from his master, hoarded it away, and realized no benefit from it.

A balanced individual learns that society repays those who contribute to it. Those who sow abundantly reap abundantly.

SOCIAL BALANCE AT HOME

Social balance begins at home. We all know workaholics who spend 24 hours a day thinking about their careers, their businesses or their hobbies, neglecting to nurture the human relationships that provide the foundation for happiness.

Sometimes marriage partners become so absorbed in their careers that they neglect each other. Their marriages slowly dissolve until one day they realize that nothing is left but a hollow shell.

One executive, who was in a business partnership with her husband, described the process this way:

> *Our family income was going up every year. We were considered the new wonder kids in our town. . . . We moved into a bigger house. It should have been great, right? But we never sought each other's company. We were already saturated. We were both working hard, but I was in the worst mode of crisis management. Sometimes I couldn't get home until 7 or 8 p.m. . . . There was a fundamental moment in this time when I chose the business over the marriage. I just didn't know it, and if I could go back in time, I would do it differently. . . The strain, the urgency to move the business forward, and the neglect of the family seem to be endemic to entrepreneurs.*[1]

Some people obsess on television or sports instead of the job. The results are similar. A family is like a house plant, in need of constant watering.

People who are truly successful take time to nurture their relationships with spouses and children. The payoff is in solid support from the home front when things get tough in business and careers.

If you consistently miss your children's plays and recitals, never show up at sports events in which they take part, and have no time to get to know their teachers, you need to restore some social balance. If you never have time to sit down and talk heart to heart with your spouse, if you consistently forget birthdays and anniversaries, and feel too harried and tense to say "I love you," you need to restore some balance.

Meal time is an excellent time to knit family relationships.

Playwright Israel Horovitz could recall fond memories of the Sunday dinners in his family, when relatives and friends were always invited over.

"My mother's side of the family told jokes, and we all rolled up and laughed," he said. "My father's side sat quietly and told impressive success stories." In his own marriage, Horovitz continued the pattern.[2]

The family dinner has been neglected all too often in the rush of modern society. Working mothers often lament that they don't have the time to interact with their families over dinner. One survey showed that 77% of working mothers do all the work in preparing dinner and 64% do all the cleaning up.

Unfair?

You bet, but it also represents a missed opportunity. Bringing husband and kids into the kitchen is an excellent way for the family to share time and activities.

Surveys also show that among families with children under 18 at home, 42% leave the television set on while eating.

No wonder family members feel isolated from each other. Meal time is an excellent time for family members to share the interesting and exciting things that happened in their lives during the day. Local and national issues can be discussed, with children being invited to submit their own views on matters of interest to them.

Unmarried people, too, need family closeness. If you're unmarried and living away from your parents, you can still cultivate a closeness with friends and relatives who have had a significant impact on your life. If you don't have such friends, go out and cultivate them!

TURNING REJECTS INTO WINNERS

Ira Pollard did, and it restored meaning and prosperity to his life. As head coach at a religious school in Tuscaloosa, Alabama, he led his team to the state championship in its division.

But his wife had divorced him, and the headmaster of his school said divorced people couldn't remain on the staff.

At first, Pollard went into depression. But he found a way out of it.

He thought, "What if I started my own team, made up of kids rejected by other teams?"

Pollard dreamed his dream, made his plans and took action. He formed a basketball team of youngsters who had been rejected by other teams. Some were too short, some were too slow, and some were too rowdy. But they made Pollard's team, which he called the Tuscaloosa Eagles. Pollard drilled them daily, and his athletes caught his enthusiasm. Three of his "rejects" went on to win basketball scholarships.

Pollard later remarried and opened a jewelry store in Mississippi. But he still devoted his free time to putting together new teams. When he was between families, he recruited his own, and his efforts helped boost him toward success.[3]

SOCIAL BALANCE IN THE COMMUNITY

Beyond the family lies the community. Successful people make it a point to become active in their communities. They show up in service clubs and volunteer organizations such as rescue squads and fire departments. They coach community-league athletic teams. They become active with Girl Scouts, Boy Scouts and other youth organizations.

They also take the lead in addressing local needs. Every community has needs that are not being met. There may be an environmental problem that needs addressing. There may be a need for a shelter for battered spouses. The young people may need more recreational facilities. Your neighborhood may need to unite to meet a challenge from undesirable development on its fringes.

If you perceive such a need, become involved in addressing it. Your efforts in community service will mark you as a concerned leader and will pave the way toward success in other endeavors. It will give you a sense of connectedness with others that will go a long way toward satisfying your need for social balance.

Authors James M. Kouzes and Barry Z. Posner polled more than 7,500 American business managers and asked them what qualities they admired in their leaders. Among them were the abilities to inspire, to understand the perspectives of others, to stand up for what you believe, and to speak with passion.

If you cultivate these qualities, you will be known to the people in your community, they will look to you for leadership, and you will be a vital part of society.

The local community is the forge in which national and world leaders are shaped and formed. Even the path to the White House starts in your own neighborhood. Harry Truman was a postmaster before he was president. Lyndon Johnson was a school teacher. William McKinley was both a postal clerk and a country school teacher. All of them rose to the presidency by becoming actively involved in their communities.

In today's society, no one has to be a loner. But to establish social connections, you have to reach out. Usually, you don't have to reach very far. Find some interest that appeals to you and look for an organization built around that interest. Join it, and you will soon find yourself in the midst of a social network.

Service clubs such as Rotary, the Lions, Kiwanis, Sertoma, Jaycees and the Civitans offer excellent opportunities for you to meet other success-oriented people, to cultivate their friendships and to create networks of supporters to help you as you move toward the goals you have set.

Many people looking for meaning in their lives find it by losing themselves in causes greater than they are. Look for a cause that touches you deeply. It may be preserving a local historical treasure from the wrecking ball. It may be creating jobs for people who are unemployed or underemployed. It may be finding solutions to problems of drug abuse and violence in your community. It may be improving the school system. Worthy causes abound. Find one that inspires you and lose yourself in it.

Keep matters in perspective, of course. If the values you identified in Chapter Three include a warm and stable family, you'll need to give that top priority. But strong family values thrive best in a stable, supportive community, and such a community can't exist without the efforts of people willing to devote themselves unselfishly to causes greater than they are.

SOCIAL BALANCE IN THE WORK PLACE

Social connections are important in the work place as well. I'm not talking about conversations around the water cooler or in the company cafeteria. Successful people become known throughout the organization where they work. Their interests extend beyond their own work stations. They find out what happens upstream from them and downstream. They know the people in other departments and at other levels. They not only know their jobs; they also know the company.

The people who work for a company need to have the same sense of belonging as do people who live in a community. A business organization is, after all, a community of people working toward common objectives.

In a healthy work environment, people feel a loyalty toward the company akin to the loyalty they feel toward their home towns or their alma maters. This feeling of community in the work place should be one of the factors you look for when choosing a place to work.

This loyalty toward the company will serve you well in the team environment that is becoming the norm for progressive business organizations. It will help you to see things from the company's perspective and not just from the vantage point of your work station.

It will also help you do the networking that often makes the difference between a star performer and a mediocrity.

Jerry Wind, a marketing professor at Wharton, asked 300 business executives what skills were needed in the corporate work place. Among the top ones was the ability to "figure out what information they need and where to get it."[4]

A study conducted in the Bell Labs Switching Systems Business Unit supports Wind's finding. It revealed that the difference between star performers and their run-of-the-mill colleagues did not lie in talent or intelligence. It lay in the work strategies they followed. Among the most important differences between the standouts and the mediocrities was their concept of networking. Both the star performers and the mediocrities recognized the advantage of sharing their expertise with others who needed it and asking for help when they needed the expertise of someone else.

Star performers, however, created their networks *before* they needed the expertise. Run-of-the-mill performers waited until they had a problem before looking for someone who could help them.

Star performers also reached out for responsibility beyond their job descriptions, and were more willing to volunteer for additional activities. They were also more vigorous in promoting new ideas.

These are the same qualities that distinguish community leaders from passive followers. Look upon your business organization as a community, and cultivate relationships there the same way you would cultivate them among your neighbors and in the service organizations to which you belong.

SOCIAL BALANCE IN LEISURE ACTIVITIES

Not all our social connections have to be dead serious, of course. All of us need to feel that we're part of a group in which we can relax and be ourselves. In the presence of like-minded friends, we can exchange pleasantries, talk shop, talk golf, or just keep silent if we want.

Your colleagues at work can be a fertile source of friendships of this type, but don't confine your friendships to the work place. Cultivate friends in other walks of life. These friendships will broaden your perspective and open up new opportunities for growth.

Develop interests that have no direct connection with your job. Take up a hobby or a sport. Then seek out others who share your interest. You'll soon begin to build a network of friendships that will prove valuable in ways you can't anticipate.

BECOME A KNOWLEDGEABLE PERSON

Whether you're in a business, family or community setting, your social skills will be greatly enhanced if you become a cultivator of knowledge.

I'm not suggesting that you memorize the encyclopedia. But a well-rounded fund of knowledge will help you become an interesting conversationalist, which in turn will help you cultivate the network of friends so vital to your success.

Take time out during the day to scan your local newspaper. Clip out or tear out articles of particular interest, so that you can go back and read them at your leisure. Read a national news magazine as well. Use television as an information as well as an entertainment medium. Televised news magazines and news commentaries can make fascinating as well as useful viewing.

Adopt a global perspective. The business environment is becoming more and more globalized, and companies will be seeking out people who understand other cultures.

As **_Fortune_** magazine noted, thinking globally "rarely means mastering 22 ways to shake hands in Romania. More often, it's a true appreciation of how differently—and equally well — things get done in other parts of the world, and how you had better take steps to understand this deeply".

Learn a foreign language. It's a major asset if you plan to sell in other countries. But it's also a plus in an increasingly multi-cultural America.[5]

Whatever the goals you've set, remember that success can never be a solitary pursuit. The more people you know and the smoother your relations with them, the greater your chances of attaining your goals.

Chapter Fourteen

Get Ready Spiritually

Great persons are they who see that the spiritual is stronger than any material force.

—Ralph Waldo Emerson.

Many people define success in terms of their material possessions. To be successful is to own a large, expensive home, with swimming pool, hot tub and an entertainment center fit for captivating royalty. Add to that a vacation home by the shore, a luxury yacht, and two or three automobiles, including a high-powered sports car, a luxury sedan and perhaps an upscale sports-utility van.

Not many people can rise to such heights of affluence, but these artifacts populate the dreams of millions.

It's all right to dream of these things, and it's all right to acquire them if your dreams take you that far.

THE GREATEST MAN WAS THE POOREST

But you won't find true happiness in these material possessions alone. And success is an empty attainment if it doesn't bring happiness.

Elvis Presley is an example of someone who had it all: a fine mansion, every luxury money could buy, and the adulation of millions. He was so saturated with money that he could buy a luxury car for a total stranger as a gesture of generosity.

Yet, in the end, he died in despair.

In contrast, as Ralph Waldo Emerson points out, "The greatest man in history was the poorest."

Though Jesus Christ had no home of his own, few material possessions beyond the clothes he wore, and no army or work force at his command, he was able to proclaim success on the eve of his trial and execution: "Be of good cheer; I have overcome the world."

Despite his material poverty, Jesus had created a spiritual legacy that would transform the world and result in immeasurable joy for himself and those who followed him — even in the midst of suffering.

Elvis Presley's tragic end was not the result of an evil life. He brought pleasure to millions, and millions yet unborn will probably enjoy his music and his movies.

But his life was lacking in its spiritual dimension.

INSPIRATION ENTERS THROUGH THE SPIRITUAL SIDE

The spiritual dimension is that which touches the core of your being. You gain access to it through the intuitive right side of your brain.

When you have spiritual balance, you are open to inspiration — that mysterious source of creativity that has been behind every great accomplishment.

"The great decisions of human life have, as a rule, far more to do with the instincts and other mysterious unconscious factors than with conscious will and well-meaning reasonableness," wrote Carl Jung, the renowned behaviorist. Jung explains:

> We should not pretend to understand the world only by the intellect; we apprehend it just as much by feeling. Therefore the judgment of the intellect is, at best, only half of truth, and must, if it be honest, also come to an understanding of its inadequacy.

George Santayana, the Spanish-born writer and philosopher, phrased it more poetically:

> It is not wisdom to be only wise,
> And on the inward vision close the eyes,
> But it is wisdom to believe the heart,
> Columbus found a world, and had no chart,

Save one that faith deciphered in the skies;
To trust the soul's invincible surmise
Was all his science and his only art.

In other words, it was faith in an inward vision that enabled Columbus to discover America, and not cold, calculated logic. Columbus, after all, didn't know where he was going when he started out, didn't know where he was when he got there, and didn't know where he had been when he returned. But he followed his "invincible surmise" that the earth was round and became an indelible part of history.

EINSTEIN'S SPIRITUAL SIDE

For me, my spirituality is founded on my firm belief in the teachings of my Lord, Jesus Christ. Some, though, feel that you don't have to be deeply involved in religion to be a spiritual person.

Albert Einstein was not a religious person in the usual sense of the word, but he was deeply spiritual. As he put it:

To know that what is impenetrable to us really exists, manifesting itself as the highest wisdom and the most radiant beauty, which our dull faculties can comprehend only in the most primitive forms — this knowledge, this feeling, is at the center of true religiousness. In this sense, and in this sense only, I belong to the ranks of the devoutly religious men.

To be spiritually balanced is to experience a level of joy and satisfaction that is unimaginable to those who think only in material terms. As philosopher Bertrand Russell observed, people who live only in the world of logic "know too much and feel too little. At least we feel too little of those creative emotions from which a good life springs."

Such people, wrote Emerson, are like scientists who comprehend only the scientific aspects of growing things and "love not the flower they pluck, and know it not, and all their botany is Latin names."

Emerson brilliantly captures the difference between a spiritual-minded and a strictly materialistic-minded person:

> *To the dull mind all nature is leaden. To the illumined mind the whole world burns and sparkles with light.*

To launch your actions toward true success, you need to tap into these wells of inspiration that can set your world on fire and make it sparkle with light.

SUGGESTIONS FOR ACHIEVING SPIRITUAL BALANCE

Here are some suggestions for achieving the spiritual balance that makes it all possible:

♦ *Value intangibles.*

That's another way of saying "Stop and smell the roses."

237

Remember that tangibles such as money and property are not truly ends, but are means toward an end. As Santayana noted, "Happiness is the only sanction of life; where happiness fails, existence remains a mad and lamentable experiment."

When your goal in life is true happiness, then, as Stanford scholar Michael Ray observes, "money and profit are no longer that important. They're a way to keep score, but if . . . you go for money and that's all, when you get it, there's nothing there."[1]

Einstein maintained that the great technical strides of mankind are meaningless apart from their effects on the human conditions. He wrote:

> *Concern for man himself and his fate must always form the chief interest of all technical endeavors . . . in order that the creations of our mind shall be a blessing and not a curse to mankind. Never forget this in the midst of your diagrams and equations.*
>
> *Among the intangibles we can value are love, joy, peace, longsuffering, kindness, goodness, faithfulness, meekness and self-control. These are the nine biblical "fruits of the spirit" that, when cultivated, can bring pleasure and fulfillment to life. And fulfillment, for me, is eternally more satisfying than mere happiness.*

♦ *Cultivate a sense of wonderment.*

"Two things fill the mind with ever-increasing wonder and awe the more often and the more intensely the mind of thought is drawn to them," wrote philosopher Immanuel Kant: "the starry heavens above me and the moral law within me."

There's nothing so awe-inspiring as the sky on a clear, smog-free night. Oscar Hammerstein, the great Broadway lyricist, called it "a dark blue curtain . . . pinned by the stars to the sky," and numbered it among "100 million miracles."

His estimate is conservative. We can see about 5,000 stars with the naked eye, but they exist by the trillions. Our middle-sized galaxy, the Milky Way, contains 100 billion of them, and the universe contains billions of galaxies. Most of those stars are at least as large as our sun, and many are much larger.

Each of them glows with the energy of billions of thermonuclear explosions. When we look at the heavens and contemplate the enormity of what is out there, we can't help but feel awe: a sense that we're a part of something much greater than ourselves.

The grandeur of mountains, the vastness of the sea, the exquisite geometry of a snowflake, and the incredible complexity of a living cell can all provide us with a sense of wonderment. Even everyday objects, when viewed through the spirit, can inspire wonder. As Walt Whitman put it, "I believe a leaf of grass is no less than the journey-work of the stars."

Contemplate these things, and you'll nourish your spiritual dimension recognizing that God has truly entrusted us with a beautiful creation.

◆ *Ask fundamental questions.*

Did the universe begin with a "big bang"? If so, was it planned or did it occur by accident? And what happened before the big bang?

If the universe is constantly expanding, will it eventually contract? And if it does, will time run backward?

If there were only one object in creation, could it move?

What would it be like to travel at the speed of light?

Fundamental questions such as these provided the starting points for Einstein's mental exploration of the nature of time and space. One of the questions he asked was "Why don't we feel gravity when we fall?"

Ask such questions, not necessarily with the idea of coming up with scientifically correct answers, but for the purpose of expanding your mind into the awe-inspiring reaches of reality.

◆ *Turn your imagination loose.*

"The debt we owe to imagination is incalculable," wrote Carl Jung. When we enter the world of fantasy, we set our minds free from the constraints of what is possible. Thus freed, they can transport us into the land where dreams come true, and can even show us how to make the dreams come true.

♦ *Cultivate a sense of place in time.*

"People who grow up without a sense of how yesterday has affected today are unlikely to have a strong sense of how today affects tomorrow," wrote Lynne V. Cheney. "It is only when we become conscious of the flow of time that the consequences of action — whether it is taking drugs or dropping out of school — become a consideration. It is only when we have perspective on our lives that motives besides immediate gratification can come into play."[2]

Spiritually balanced people don't live in the past, but they are aware of their place in the flow of time, and cultivate an appreciation for the contributions the past has made to the present.

Contemplating the endless span of time also fills us with a sense of awe. The question of where we came from and how we got here has intrigued thinking people for millenniums, and has inspired some of the most breathtaking leaps of insight.

♦ *Accumulate good memories.*

"There is nothing higher and stronger and more wholesome and useful for life in later years than some good memory, especially a memory connected with childhood, with home," wrote Feodor Dostoevsky, the great Russian writer. "If a man carries many such memories with him into life, he is safe to the end of his days, and if we have only one good memory left in our hearts, even that may sometime be the means of saving us."

241

The way to accumulate good memories is to dream toward the future, act in harmony with the dream, and savor the fulfillment. The good moments of the present are the good memories you will carry into your future.

♦ *Pursue happiness.*

Happiness comes to those who go after it. "Make up your mind to be happy," was one of the daily dozen items in Robert Louis Stevenson's personal creed. And, as Abraham Lincoln observed, "Any man can be just about as happy as he makes up his mind to be."

Playwright George Bernard Shaw found happiness by living life to its fullest.

"I rejoice in life for its own sake," he wrote. "Life is no brief candle to me. It's a sort of splendid torch which I've got to hold up for the moment and I want to make it burn as brightly as possible before handing it to future generations."

Happiness is something you can obtain by helping others to become happy.

A brokerage house may seem like an unlikely place for this philosophy to emerge, but Judith Resnick, chairman and CEO of Dabney/Resnick & Wagner Inc., of Los Angeles has made it a part of her corporate culture.

"If you can get your employees to play well with each other, share their toys, remember the golden rule, you'll be okay," she told an interviewer.

♦ *Involve yourself in the arts.*

America is awakening to the arts, which may be replacing sports as the most popular way of spending leisure time.

Poetry, music, literature, sculpture, painting and the dance are all forms of expression that spring from the human spirit. They speak to something deep inside us. Each is the product of inspiration and each in turn has the power to inspire us.

♦ *Keep a positive, open mind.*

"The bigoted, the narrow-minded, the stubborn, and the perpetually optimistic have all stopped learning," wrote Bill Crosby in his book, **_Quality is Free._**

We obtain spiritual strength by reaching out to understand our fellow humans. Love is the most positive force on earth, and each of us can cultivate it.

How can we cultivate love toward those whom we instinctively dislike or resent?

By "faking it till we make it." If you *practice* the principle of love, you will soon find your feelings taking their cue from your actions.

You also cultivate love by banishing hatred. Hatred is the most destructive force on earth. It does the most damage to those who harbor it.

"Hating people," said Harry Emerson Fosdick, "is like burning your house down to get rid of a rat."

◆ *Stay young.*

You don't do this with face lifts, magic potions and fountains of youth. Youth is an inner quality, not an external one. As Samuel Ullman puts it:

> *Youth is not a time of life; it's a state of mind; it is not a matter of rosy cheeks, red lips and supple knees; it is a matter of the will, a quality of the imagination, a vigor of the emotions; it is the freshness of the deep springs of life.*
>
> *Whether 60 or 16, there is in every human being's heart the lure of wonder, the unfailing child-like appetite of what's next and the joy of the game of living. In the center of your heart and my heart there is a wireless station: so long as it receives messages of beauty, hope, cheer, courage and power from men and from the Infinite, so long you are young.*

LOOK BEYOND THE ARTIFACTS

Sometimes, in this materialistic world, we lose sight of the spiritual side of our natures. We build our lives around the artifacts that bring us convenience: refrigerators, microwaves, central air; automatic garage-door openers, automatic transmissions, automatic door locks; computers, video games and VCRs.

Sometimes, amid the pace of change, we lose our spiritual perspective. How do we regain it?

Start with the fact that the verities we salute so reverently today are mists in the night, wisps fated to dissipate before winds of planned obsolescence. Today's young people will live for a while in the world of their elders, which already is like none that has existed before. They will change it dramatically into their world, for the distinguishing feature of the 20th century has been rapid change; impermanence.

In the preceding century, the sum total of a parent's knowledge could be passed on to son or daughter with the reasonable expectation that it would be useful and relevant. The values and morals held by the preceding generation would hold up for the succeeding age.

Today, the frontier of knowledge moves so rapidly that yesterday is obsolete before it becomes a memory. Today's pearls of wisdom are tomorrow's outdated concepts. Today's social environment is tomorrow's old-fashioned society. Today's behavioral standards are tomorrow's outmoded morality. Today's Madonna is tomorrow's Rosemary Clooney.

And so I offer these observations to put things in perspective:

- ♦ *Happiness is not the same thing as having a ball.*

Life is a series of highs and lows, and the measure of happiness is the plateau that lies between them. People who make fun their goal in life may end up having a ball but being miserable in the process. True happiness comes with the feeling of being at harmony with self, with God and with fellow humans.

♦ *Machines are the artifacts of our culture, and should not be mistaken for its substance.*

Machines make life more convenient and often more fun, but the mind that becomes overly absorbed in gadgets may lose out on many of the pleasures that enrich the human experience.

Music, poetry, drama, dance, comedy, all have benefited by the technical progress of mankind. The piano, the electric keyboard, the stereo system, movies, television, and other technical artifacts have enhanced our enjoyment of these arts. But music, literature and drama are not the products of machines. They are the products of the human mind, connected to other human minds by centuries of accumulated knowledge.

To know the operation of a machine is good, but that knowledge is like a dangling, disconnected wire unless it is accompanied by a knowledge of the historical, philosophical and intellectual processes that have brought us to the machine.

The people who lived before us were not less intelligent than we; they simply lacked the fund of knowledge that we inherited. The Neanderthal man couldn't build a car, because he didn't have the tools to make it. So he started inventing the tools so that we could build automobiles.

Learn about automobiles — and about hardware and software and microchips, if these terms are still relevant to the technology of your age. But learn also about Alexander, the Greek general who wept because there were no more worlds to conquer, and Cincinnatus, the Roman general who sought nothing more than the peace and contentment of his farm after he had saved Rome from invaders. Learn about Chang An, which was the capital of a great empire in China when Rome was a rural village, and Carthage, the city that challenged Rome for supremacy and was reduced to a barren wasteland. Learn about Jefferson the prophet of freedom, and Marx, the progenitor of tyranny; about Homer and Virgil, Shakespeare and Wordsworth, Tolstoy and Dostoevsky, Dante and Milton. And learn about Ptolemy, Bacon, Newton and Einstein, who slowly built up the concept of the universe on which the latest technology rests, and who did it with the most sophisticated tool of all — the human brain, aided by artifacts scarcely more complex than pen and paper.

♦ *The last shall be first and the first shall be last.*

You will be taught, as you pursue higher education, or as you progress in your chosen calling, how to look out for your own interests and to pursue opportunities aggressively. But even more important is knowing when to sacrifice your own interests for the good of others. People who invariably put themselves first will find that others tend to put them last, and they will end up as lonely failures.

TWO GREAT PREACHERS

If you have studied English literature, you know of John Donne, the great 17th century poet and preacher. I should like to share with you the wisdom of Donne and of one other great preacher whose words will ring with eloquence and relevance long after today's media and entertainment idols have been ignored as cultural oddities. Donne wrote:

> *No man is an island, entire of itself; every man is a piece of the continent, a part of the main; if a clod be washed away by the sea, Europe is the less, as well as if a promontory were, as well as if a manor of thy friends or of thine own were; any man's death diminishes me, because I am involved in mankind; and therefore never send to know for whom the bell tolls; it tolls for thee.*

The other preacher, the greatest one of them all, condensed into 15 words — in the English translation — the best formula yet advanced for human peace and happiness: "As ye would that men do to you, do ye also to them likewise."

These truths do not change. They were valid when your grandparents lived and their parents before them. They will not be rendered obsolete by advancing knowledge of this waning century and the one emerging. As guides to future happiness, their value exceeds that of anything that has emerged from the laboratories of Silicon Valley, the studios of Hollywood, or the lecture halls of MIT. In an age in which most things that glitter are plastic, they are nuggets of gold. Treasure them.

Chapter Fifteen

Get Set

I have found enthusiasm for work to be the most priceless ingredient in any recipe for success.

— Samuel Goldwynn

At the call "Get set!" the racer's muscles tense like a taut spring ready to be released.

As the tension gives the spring motivation, so the tense muscles give the runner a source of starting energy.

As you prepare to follow your action plan, you too need to build up a store of energy to propel you toward your goals.

You can give yourself that starting boost by following these steps:

1. Cultivate morale sources.
2. Build up positive stress.
3. Manage negative stress.

CULTIVATE MORALE SOURCES

You can't act enthusiastically when your morale is low. Neither can you act creatively. Research by Dr. Marian Diamond, an eminent authority on the brain, shows that when your morale is low day in and day out, the creative part of your brain becomes thinner.

When your morale is high day in and day out, the creative part of your brain thickens. This means that your ability to think creatively is tied directly to your morale.

Morale is influenced by the presence of endorphins in your brain.

Endorphins are substances that work on the same segments of the brain as morphine. They kill pain and elevate the mood.

Our bodies secrete endorphins. Some of us are better than others at secreting them. People who grow up in stable households with warm, supportive parents usually have well-developed capacities for secreting endorphins. Cuddling and hugging a child stimulates the production of endorphins. A child who gets lots of physical affection develops a strong capacity for producing endorphins, and this capacity continues into adulthood. A child so nurtured has a much better chance of growing into a confident, optimistic adult.

If you were not fortunate enough to grow up in such an atmosphere, don't despair. You can develop sources of morale, too.

Here are some sources of outside help that can FIRE up production of morale-lifting beta endorphins.

Family closeness
Involvement in a cause
Relationships with supportive groups
Exercise

FAMILY CLOSENESS

When we're in the friendly presence of people we love dearly, our bodies secrete endorphins. In the presence of these loved ones, we feel easy and secure. When we're separated from them, we feel depressed.

If your work has caused you to neglect close relationships, take time to re-establish them.

Hugs are potent generators of endorphins. The next time you hug someone you love, notice the warm, upbeat feeling it gives you. If you're not in the habit of hugging your children, your spouse or your significant other, take up the habit. Make it a warm, cheek-to-cheek, loving embrace. It will make you and your hugging partner feel better.

If you don't have a spouse or significant other, take time to contact parents, siblings, aunts, uncles, nieces or nephews regularly for friendly chats and, if possible, an exchange of hugs.

INVOLVEMENT IN A CAUSE

The knowledge that you're making a difference can give your morale a strong boost. Find a cause you believe in strongly, and put your best efforts into advancing it.

RELATIONSHIPS WITH SUPPORTIVE GROUPS

All of us need the companionship of friends with whom we can relax and be ourselves. These friends needn't come from our work-place colleagues. They can be anyone with whom we feel free to let down our hair.

When you begin embarking on your action plan, share your goals with a few close friends, and ask them to share their goals with you. Make it a point to meet with them regularly and, in an easy, informal atmosphere, share with them your successes and your challenges. Their encouragement will provide you with a potent morale boost.

EXERCISE

Vigorous exercise causes the body to produce endorphins. These endorphins are the source of the "jogger's high." A program of regular exercise will pump a healthy supply of endorphins into your bloodstream. Don't overdo it, though. People can become addicted to exercise.

BUILD UP POSITIVE STRESS

Stress gets a bad rap around the work place, but you should know that there is good stress and there's bad stress.

Good stress can be used like the tension in a bowstring. Unless you stress the bow and the string, your arrow won't fly straight to its mark.

A person who is experiencing no stress is also experiencing no challenge. And people who are not challenged will not exert themselves to succeed. Unchallenged people are bored and unmotivated.

Challenged people are excited and ready for action. They're like a talented, well-trained team going into a championship game. The challenge of winning fills the team members with an exciting tension that puts the edge on their performance, causing them to play at their best — and win.

PUT YOURSELF IN YOUR VISION

Your vision and your action plan should fill you with positive stress that impels you to move toward your goals. That's why it's important to create an exciting vision. An effective vision arouses your passions. It sets in front of you a future so enticing that you can taste it.

You should be able to see yourself in the vision. In your mind's eye, picture yourself as you will be when the vision has been fulfilled. If you can't see yourself in the vision, it won't have drawing power. The key to motivation is identity. If you can't identify personally with the vision and goals, you won't be able to generate sufficient interest and enthusiasm to bring them to reality.

UPGRADE YOUR SELF-ESTIMATE

Some people dream exciting dreams, but never bring them out of dreamland.

Often, the reason is that the person mistakes an exciting dream for an impossible dream.

There's an unconscious rating process that we go through when we're sizing up tasks. We think of the task in comparison to our own capacities.

If we think the task is bigger than we are, we become discouraged and we don't try.

If we think the task is beneath our capacities, we're bored by it, and we bypass it.

But if we think the task matches our capacities, we're likely to wade into it.

The key to motivating yourself is to upgrade your estimate of your own capacities. If the dream excites you, you can achieve it. If it were beyond your reach, it wouldn't excite you. So when you face a major challenge, give your estimate of your capabilities an upward revision.

THE DOCTRINE OF "AND THEN SOME"

Follow the doctrine of "and then some."

Have you ever eaten until you were so full you felt that you couldn't eat another bite? But then when the server came around with a tantalizing dessert, you were able to make room for it, weren't you?

You ate all you could hold "and then some."

Have you ever been in a race and come to the point that you thought you couldn't run another step? Then you saw a rival overtaking you, and you forced yourself to pick up the pace and run to the finish.

You gave it all you had "and then some."

Has your schedule ever been so full that you knew you couldn't find time to do anything else? And then the boss came in and said, "I'd like for you to take on just one more project this month. There's a nice bonus in it for you if you can handle it."

You did all the work you could handle "and then some."

When you're sizing up your capacities, allow for the "and then some." The "and then some" provides you with positive stress that enables you to meet the challenge — and then some.

USING PAIN AND PLEASURE

Positive stress enables you to overcome the inertia that tends to keep you in a rut.

People stay in ruts because it takes less effort to follow the rut than to get out of it.

But two things can cause you to get out of the rut: Those two things are pain and pleasure.

When the pain of staying in the rut becomes appreciably greater than the pain of getting out of it, you'll get out of it.

When getting out of the rut offers you appreciably more pleasure than staying in the rut, you'll get out of it.

Both the pain and the pleasure represent positive stress.

Notice my insertion of the word "appreciably." There's an inertia in our lives that tends to keep us going in the same direction until we encounter a strong, substantial reason to change directions.

This inertia can be a healthy thing, because it keeps us from changing directions with every wayward wind of fancy. Thomas Jefferson expressed it well in the American Declaration of Independence:

> . . . (E)xperience hath shown that mankind are more disposed to suffer, while evils are sufferable, than to

right themselves by abolishing the forms to which they are accustomed.

The American colonies were willing to remain in their colonial rut with England so long as the mother country allowed them reasonable leeway to manage their internal affairs. Only after they felt the pinch of the Stamp Act and other economic and political measures did the colonies rise in rebellion, and only after they were convinced that they could never achieve the rights they wanted within the British Empire did they seek independence. The heady prospect of freedom and the worrysome pain of economic repression provided twin doses of stress, which enabled them to overcome their inertia.

You encounter the same kind of decision-making in your daily life. You stay in an unchallenging job because the daily routine is comfortable and you feel that finding another job isn't worth the inconvenience and adjustments that might be necessary. But when an obnoxious boss starts adding daily pain and insult to your life; when the cost of living rises much faster than your income; and when the demands of the job disrupt your family and social life, the pain becomes great enough to motivate you to change.

On the other hand, a lucrative offer from another company might very well promise you enough pleasure to cause you to make the change.

You can provide that motivation by giving yourself a stake in the changes.

You may want a larger house, but the higher payments would pinch your budget on your present income. You might have to give up your second car or your boat. So your inclination is to remain in your present small house.

What would happen if you signed a contract on a larger, more comfortable and more expensive house?

The pain of making the payments might motivate you to increase your earnings through increased job performance, or a through finding a better job.

Suppose your goal is to win the free trip to Hawaii that your company is offering as an incentive. You can put pleasurable tension into your life by obtaining travel brochures and videos on Hawaii, planning your itinerary, shopping for vacation clothes, and acting as if the trip had already been won.

If you don't win the prize, you will at least have enhanced your performance and will be starting on a higher plane when it's time to compete for the next incentive prize.

GIVE YOURSELF A STAKE

The most valuable people to a business organization are those who believe that they have a stake in the company's profitability. Such people craft personal visions that are in alignment with the organizational vision. They make the organization's goals their goals, take pride in the company's successes and look for ways to overcome obstacles to that success. They refer to the organization as "we" and not as "they."

THE STRESS OF PRIDE

Let pride become a source of positive stress for you. Make it a matter of pride to achieve the results you seek. When your pride is at stake, you'll work doubly hard to avoid injury to your ego.

One way of putting pride on your side is to advertise your vision and goals. Put them in writing and display them prominently around your home and work area. Then you'll be motivated to prove to your supporters and critics alike that you can do what you've put your mind to do.

FEAR AS POSITIVE STRESS

Even something as negative as fear can be a positive motivator.

"Depend on it sir," said Dr. Samuel Johnson, "When a man knows he is to be hanged in a fortnight, it concentrates his mind wonderfully."

You don't have to face the gallows to have a healthy fear. Many an entrepreneur has found that in those moments when everything was at stake, when the fate of the business seemed to hang on every decision, the most creative ideas surface.

Success in almost any undertaking requires that you engage in risk-taking, and with each risk comes the element of fear. How you respond to the fear makes the difference between success and failure. If you cower before it, running for cover at the first hint of disaster, you will fail. If you meet it boldly, letting it motivate you to action, you will succeed.

Benjamin Franklin told his fellow patriots at the signing of the Declaration of Independence: "We must all hang together, or assuredly we shall all hang separately."

The delegates who signed their names to the document were opening themselves to the charge of treason — a capital crime. They affixed their signatures, and this act of bold risk-taking wonderfully concentrated their minds. The colonies won their independence against great odds.

You can beat the odds, too, by engaging in healthy risk-taking, and acting boldly to surmount the risk.

"You cannot surrender to fear, but you can use it as a kind of fuel," said Jose Torres. "Once you learn to control fear — to make it work for you — it will become one of your best friends."

MANAGE NEGATIVE STRESS

Just as positive stress can be the spring that propels you toward success, so negative stress can be the brake that stops you in your tracks.

As you embark on your action plans, learn to take control of the negative stress in your life. You won't be able to eliminate it, because we don't live in a perfect world. But successful people learn how to minimize it and to live with it when it's inevitable.

Stress is your body's way of responding to a challenge. When primitive people perceived threats to their safety, fear sent signals to their brains and the brain responded by stimulating the production of energizing substances. The body suddenly became charged with energy. The primitive person could use that energy to flee from the enemy or to subdue it in a fight. Either way, the excess energy was used up through physical exertion.

In modern society, we rarely face physical threats. The challenges are more likely to be of a mental or emotional nature. Still, our brains respond by energizing our bodies. Just as auto racers rev their engines in preparation for quick starts, so your brain "revs" your response system in preparation for decisive action.

When the decisive action fails to come, we experience unrelieved stress. And just as constant racing of an auto engine will result in premature wear, so constant stress can result in premature physical and emotional damage to humans.

ACTION RELIEVES STRESS

Your action plan itself will eliminate a great deal of stress. Action relieves stress, and your plan provides a blueprint for action. We feel stressed out when we feel that we're not in control of events. We control the stress by taking control of events. Following an action plan puts you in control.

Many people give up on various areas of their lives. When their marriages encounter problems, they stop trying to make them work and let events take their course. The course often leads to divorce court — a caldron of stress.

When bills start mounting faster than their incomes, they stop trying to control credit-card spending and let events take their course. The course often leads to bankruptcy court, and a mountain of stress.

When work on the job piles up faster than they can handle it, they stop trying to control it and let events take their course. They may end up taking work home with them, or working unreasonably long hours to keep up with the flow. They're building up stress, and they're heading for burn-out or even a nervous breakdown.

Their motto, when things get out of control, is "Don't just do something; stand there!"

And the more they stand there, the more the stress piles up.

The solution to this type of stress is purposeful action. You have to decide to do something about it, make a commitment to do something about it, develop a plan and execute it.

BE HONEST; BE YOURSELF

Another safeguard against negative stress is honesty. When you engage in deception, you're constantly worried lest somebody uncover the deception.

Dishonesty can take the form of outright lies to cover up mistakes or disguise incompetence. But the more you cover up, the more there is to uncover — and the greater the chance that it will be uncovered.

Disguising incompetence doesn't alter the basic condition. But incompetence can be overcome. If you're in a job that requires talents you don't possess, don't spend your time covering up your lack of talent. Spend it looking for a job that will enable you to use the talents you *do* have. Find your congenial competencies, look for a compatible career and search out a congenial role within that career.

But don't try to be somebody you're not. Learn to like yourself for who you are and what you are. When you like yourself, you will gravitate toward people who like you. You won't have to deceive them, and you won't have to subject yourself to the stress of trying to hide your real self.

There may be some things about yourself that you don't like. If they're things you can change, change them. If you can't change them, accept them. I liked the attitude behind the message on a T-shirt I encountered one day as I was jogging around my neighborhood. The wearer was a pleasant looking woman, though she wouldn't have turned heads at Waikiki. The message read: "I'm not perfect, but parts of me are excellent."

So don't worry about imperfections that can't be changed. Remember that parts of you are excellent.

Keep reminding yourself of your attributes. When you fail to achieve an objective, remind yourself of the times when you did succeed. Celebrate those moments and give yourself the credit you're due.

EXAMINE YOUR PERCEPTIONS

Remember that stress arises from *perceived* challenges. If the cave man saw a shadow that looked like a lion, his body responded as if the shadow actually were a lion. That was his subconscious brain at work. The subconscious believes what the conscious mind perceives. The conscious mind perceived a lion, and the subconscious acted as if the perception were reality.

So when you find your stress level rising, stop and ask yourself: Is this really something worth worrying about? You may find yourself stewing all day because the boss walked past you without speaking. You engage in negative self-talk: "I must not matter much to him; I guess I don't have much of a future here."

The reality may have been that the boss was absorbed in contemplation of the company's next acquisition, and simply didn't notice you. You can't know what's on the boss's mind. Stop worrying about it.

PICK YOUR BATTLES

Sometimes the answer to a stressful situation is to walk away from it. Successful people pick their battles. When the unarmed cave man saw a lion approaching from the opposite side of the glade, he didn't charge out there and do battle with his bare hands. He made himself scarce.

That's what you need to do when you examine your circumstances objectively and determine that you're in a no-win situation. Get out of it. If you hate your job and your boss and are convinced that you're at a dead end, find another job and another boss.

When the cave man made good his escape from the lion and rushed into the camp, what was his first impulse?

To tell everybody about his experience!

We all have a need to share with others the stressful situations we encounter. That doesn't mean that we should bend every ear with accounts of our troubles and woes. But it is helpful to have a confidante you can trust, with whom you can talk over your problems with a view to achieving perspective and finding solutions. Talking it over with such a person can be a good tension-reliever. Often, after we've vented our emotions, we find that the situation wasn't as bad as we thought it was.

PUT VARIETY INTO YOUR LIFE

Sometimes stress results from following the same boring routine. It isn't hard to inject a little variety into your life. Here are some suggestions:

♦ Drive to work by a different route. The change of scenery will do you good.

♦ Find a hobby. Make it something unrelated to your job. It should be something compatible with your talents and interests that you find relaxing and pleasurable.

♦ Seek out new interests. Explore your library for subjects that interest you. Your interests may range from handicrafts to high fashion, from archaeology to astronomy. Whatever the interest, pursue it because it interests you, not because you feel obligated to pursue it.

♦ Take an evening to relax. It may be a night on the town, a quiet dinner in a relaxing setting, a live concert or play, a dinner theater, or just a movie. Make it a treat for yourself.

TEN ANTIDOTES TO STRESS

Ten simple rules will help you minimize the stress you experience daily in your personal life and your work life:

1. *Relax over breakfast.*

How often have you stolen an extra half-hour of snooze time in the morning, gulped down a glazed donut and a cup of coffee, and rushed into the swirl of traffic in a mad race with the time clock?

Try retiring early enough so that you can rise in time to enjoy a leisurely breakfast. Occasionally, arrange to meet with a friend or co-worker for a healthy breakfast before going to work. Enjoy a glass of water or fruit juice instead of coffee, tea or carbonated beverage. The breakfast will give you a good supply of energy to start the day, and the friendly conversation will leave you relaxed and alert.

2. *Organize your work.*

When you sit down each morning, make a list of things you need to do. Arrange them in order of priority. Do them one at a time. If any of them remain undone at the end of the day, carry them over to your list for tomorrow.

3. *Allow yourself to be imperfect.*

Why should you be different from anyone else? If you don't do things precisely the way you think they should be done, make note of ways you can improve. But don't dwell on the flaws in your work. Dwell on the things you did right.

4. *Don't do it all.*

Learn to say no when your plate is full of things to do. Delegate to others when it's possible. Form alliances with fellow workers so that they can pitch in when you're flooded with things to do and they're experiencing slack periods. Be willing to do the same for them.

5. *Don't take your work home with you.*

Home is for relaxing and cultivating family ties. If necessary, come in a little early or stay a little later on occasion. But plan your work so that it doesn't absorb you around the clock.

6. *Shut out unnecessary noise.*

Some work places are noisy out of necessity, and there's not much you can do about it. But if you have your own office, you may be able to reduce the noise level through the use of rugs and draperies.

Away from the job, look for ways to reduce the amount of noise to which you are subjected. Do you leave the television set on when nobody is watching it? Does the TV, radio or stereo remain on while you're eating? Could you use shrubs and fencing to shut out traffic noise? You may be surprised at the relaxing effects of an occasional interlude of quiet.

7. *Let people know what bothers you.*

There's a difference between being a constant complainer and being everybody's doormat. If people do things that constantly annoy you, let them know in a calm, respectful way. Most people don't intentionally annoy. If you let them know, they'll usually try to avoid the conduct that drives you up a wall.

8. *Take a break.*

When you take a break, make it a real break. Take some time to meditate. Ten or 15-minutes spent thinking about relaxing scenes and subjects can put you in a relaxed mood and enhance your productivity as well. Don't eat at your desk or work station. Meet a friend for lunch. Take a stroll through a quiet neighborhood, or just go window shopping.

9. *Develop stress-reduction strategies.*

Become aware of the symptoms of negative stress, and develop strategies for dealing with them when they become acute. The strategy may be nothing more complicated than pausing, putting your feet up, breathing deeply, and letting your mind meditate on relaxing topics or wander over soothing scenes.

10. *Learn to laugh.*

Nothing relieves tension better than a good, hearty laugh. Develop the ability to laugh at yourself. When you can see the humor in embarrassing situations, they cease to be stressful.

"You grow up the day you have the first real laugh — at yourself," said Ethel Barrymore. And Linda Ellerbee, the television personality who won a battle against breast cancer, found that "A good time to laugh is anytime you can."

When you stock up on morale, you're ready to respond to the "Go" signal in the action process. Make it a daily practice to attend to the things that make you feel good about yourself.

NOURISH YOUR MORALE DAILY

My late friend, Dr. Norman Vincent Peale, liked to cite the words of Dr. Jan S. Marais, chairman of The Trust Bank in Cape Town, South Africa:

> *Inspiration and motivation are exactly like nutrition. You have to keep on taking it daily, in healthy doses. Otherwise, depletion, fatigue, depression and lack of ambition and achievement will very soon manifest themselves.*

And that's no way to start executing your action plan.

Step Five

EXECUTION

Stairway To Success

Prelude to Step Five

Nothing Happens Until You Act

He who has begun has half done. Dare to be wise; begin!

— Horace

The time comes when you must put your dreams and plans into action. You know where you want to go. You've set goals to lead you to your destination. You developed strategies for attaining your goals. You've acquired the motivation. It's time to go.

The execution of your game plan is not a straight-line process. It's a spiral. The formula is this:

1. ***Act.*** Look at your life as a picture you're painting. When you begin painting a picture, you first form a mental image of what you want the finished painting to look like. That's your vision. Then you decide on the order in which you will paint the various elements of the picture. That's planning. Then you begin putting colors on the palette. That's action. You never know just what effect the colors will produce until you see them on the palette. Chances are, your initial effort won't produce the picture you envisioned, but you'll never know how different it is until you see the actual colors on the palette.

   It's that way when you begin moving toward your goals. You act. You can't be sure that your actions will have the desired results, but you'll never find out until you've acted.

2. ***Learn.*** When you've started painting your picture, you look at the colors on the palette and compare them with the picture you've visualized. Is this what you envisioned? Is it better than what you envisioned? Is it worse? If so, what did you do that made it fall short of your vision? What can you do to make it conform to your vision?

276

It's the same way when you begin moving toward a goal. You act. Then you analyze what you've done in the light of your goal. Did it take you closer to the goal? Is it missing the mark? If the results weren't what you had envisioned, then decide what you need to do to put you on track toward your goal.

3. *Apply.* Having learned from your first action, you now apply the lessons. You *act* again, this time modifying your actions in harmony with what you've learned.

4. *Learn.* After applying the lessons you learned from your first action, you stand off and look at the picture again. Did the new methods work? Did they take you closer to your goal? If not, why? What changes should you now make?

Continue this process of acting, learning and applying until you have reached the goal you set for yourself. Then focus on the next goal and repeat the spiral. Act, learn and apply.

One by one, you will reach the goals you've set, and each goal will take you closer to the fulfillment of your vision.

The starting gun is sounding. *Go!*

Chapter Sixteen

Action!

Dreams can be fact
If you act —
It's up to you.
— Oscar Hammerstein III

The time to act is now. You can't start tomorrow and you can't start "some day." "Some day" is usually a euphemism for "never."

So take out your action plan, look at your first goal, analyze your strategy for reaching it, and begin the execution.

We learned earlier that all actions are the results of thoughts and feelings.

So your first thought should be "What must I do *today* to make this happen?"

Milestones are achieved one step at a time. So decide what the first step will be, *and take it.*

Here are some pointers for getting the ball rolling:

1. *Get sound advice.*

Blind action gets you nowhere. You have to know where to direct your efforts and what will be required to see them to completion. So before you act, consult someone who has expertise in the area in which you plan to act.

Let's say your goal is to become a professional photographer. Your first action might be to set up an appointment with someone who is already a professional photographer and determine what steps you need to take. It may be going to a career-day and obtaining all the information you can on the profession.

2. *Lay the groundwork.*

You don't start a house by installing the spiral staircase. You begin by clearing the lot and laying the foundation. If you're a novice with a camera and your goal is to become a professional photographer, you don't begin by applying for a photographer's job with National Geographic. You begin by assembling the resources you need to learn photography.

Basically, you'll need three types of resources:

(a) Physical.
(b) Financial.
(c) Human.

To achieve your goal to become a photographer, for instance, you'll need, at minimum, a camera and some film. These are the physical resources that will start you toward your career.

Purchasing the camera and film will require money. Photography lessons will also require money. You'll have costs associated with processing the film and producing the photographs. You may want to subscribe to a good photography magazine. You will need financial resources to enable you to afford these things.

To become a good photographer, you'll need someone to teach you the techniques. This may mean enrolling in a photography course. It may also mean finding a mentor, or at least an established professional who can give you helpful advice. You may need models for your photographs. You may need people to help you find employment to support yourself until you can embark upon your career. These are your human resources.

Take stock of what you now have.

Do you already own a camera? Find out whether it's the kind you can use to develop your expertise. Are you able to afford the classes and equipment? If not, do what is necessary to obtain the necessary finances. Do you know someone who is a professional photographer? If not, take steps to locate someone who knows the business.

Depending upon your answers to these questions, your first action might be any of the following:

- ♦ Visit a camera store and select a good camera.

- ♦ Start a savings account to accumulate funds for a camera and related equipment.

- ♦ Search the want-ads for a job to support yourself while you're acquiring photographic skills.

- ♦ Make an appointment with a professional photographer to obtain information on career requirements and prospects.

Whatever your first step is to be, *take it today*. It may be a small step, but you can't move toward your goal until you've taken it.

3. *Stick to the timetable.*

Keep the vision glowing in the back of your mind, and keep your long-range goals in view. But concentrate your efforts on achieving the *next* immediate goal. Observe the timetable you established in your action plan, and do the things it calls for *when it calls for them.*

Set weekly goals aimed at carrying you toward your short-term objectives. Then prepare daily to-do lists that will take you toward your weekly goals. Schedule your activities around priorities: What do you need to do next to fulfill the requirements of your action plan?

Some of the things you need to do will be routine, boring, and perhaps even arduous. For example, the real-estate agent lives for the moment of closing, when the buyer pays the seller and the agent collects the commission. But before that can happen, the agent has to canvass the neighborhoods for possible listings, perhaps even going through the telephone directory in search of people with homes for sale. Then comes the advertising, the showing, the qualifying of prospects — all the grunt work that goes into a successful sale.

The successful salesperson does all these mundane things, knowing that the rewards justify the effort. When you're tempted to skip the necessary but routine tasks, remind yourself of the rewards that lie beyond them, when your vision has become a reality. This will give you the motivation to act, even when you would rather be doing something else.

4. Don't do everything yourself.

Everything you need to do requires time: either yours or someone else's. The art of time management is really the art of self management. You must decide what tasks you can handle more effectively yourself and what tasks are more effectively delegated to others.

Delegation is advisable under these circumstances:

- The task to be accomplished is time-consuming but does not require much expertise. In this case, you may conclude that your own time is too valuable to be devoted to the task. Delegate to someone whose time is less valuable than yours.

- The task requires talent or expertise beyond your level. In that case, go to the professionals.

If you're planning to send out newsletters to prospective clients or patrons, for instance, you might decide that writing the text lies within your area of expertise. But you might choose to go to a commercial printer to assure quality in the finished product. Stuffing the newsletter into envelopes is definitely within your area of expertise, but it is time-consuming and you would be better occupied in other activities. So you might delegate this task to someone else.

5. *Look for small successes.*

Nobody hits a home run every time at bat. And few hit for the distance on their first trip to the plate. It helps build confidence, though, if you can get on base with some regularity.

As you move toward your vision, keep this in mind. It isn't important that you score a major success at the outset of your venture. It *is* important, though, that you establish a *pattern* of success. When you succeed, stop and celebrate. Your subconscious mind can't distinguish between small successes and large successes. It will perceive each little accomplishment as further evidence that you are a successful person, and will bestow upon you the aura of a winner.

6. *Concentrate on opportunities.*

You'll make more headway by exploiting opportunities than you will by solving problems. Some people spend so much time dealing with petty problems that they never have time to think creatively about opportunities. Learn to recognize and correct problems while they're still in the proactive stage — that is, before they threaten to become crises. If possible, delegate these problems to others, so that you can concentrate on doing the important things.

7. *Share your knowledge and expertise.*

Everyone needs help from time to time. Create mutually beneficial relationships with others, making yourself available to help others when your talents and expertise are needed and seeking their help when you need it.

Don't be timid about asking for help. The most people can say is "no," which means you'll be no worse off than you would be if you never asked.

8. *Never approach a task tentatively.*

Go into each task with the attitude that there's no turning back. If you tell yourself, "If it doesn't work out, I'll just go back to the way things were," you'll always go back to the way things were.

9. *Think things through.*

It always helps to have a "Plan B," but Plan B should be designed to take you toward the same goal you set for Plan A.

You'll be able to stay with a task for the duration if you think it through before you undertake it. Examine the probable impact of each action you take. Think about how it will affect the goals you've set. Try to anticipate the things that might go wrong, and develop strategies for dealing with them.

10. *Clear the decks of unfinished things.*

Your life can become so full of loose ends that you're walking around in a perpetual tangle. Most of us start things and never finish them; we just leave them lying around, promising to pick them up again when we get around to it.

If you want to take purposeful action, rid yourself of this debris. Take a hard look at your unfinished projects and decide which ones will contribute to your vision and which ones are irrelevant. Make the relevant ones a part of your goals, setting deadlines for completing them. Write off the irrelevant ones. Put them in the past and move on to more meaningful activities.

When you start taking action and you see those actions taking you toward your goals, your excitement begins to quicken. You're on your way! Down the road lies your vision, waiting for you to turn it into reality. Your goals are serving as milestones. Each one takes you closer to your dream. Take them one at a time. If you act in accordance with your plan, you'll get there.

Chapter Seventeen

Learning and Applying

If at first you don't succeed, you're running about average.

—M. H. Alderson

We learn by doing.

Think about the basic skills you've acquired in life. You learned to walk by pulling yourself up, turning loose and taking a step. You fell the first time, but you got up and tried again. Each time you did it a little better than the time before. You were learning by doing.

Somebody may have *told* you how to tie your shoes, but you didn't really learn it until you had tried it yourself. You made mistakes at first, but eventually your fingers learned to do the task unconsciously.

You learned to ride a bicycle by getting on and riding it. You learned to drive a car by taking one out on the highway with an experienced teacher who could give you instructions and point out your mistakes as you drove.

PRODUCTIVE MISTAKES

With each endeavor, you started as a novice, and you learned proficiency from the mistakes you made.

It's that way in any undertaking.

When you begin taking action toward your goals, you will make mistakes. Don't worry about it. Everybody makes them. Successful people learn from theirs. They know the difference between a *productive failure* and a *non-productive success*.

In a productive failure, you don't achieve your objective, but you come away with new knowledge and understanding that will increase your chances of success on the next try. A non-productive success occurs when you achieve your objective, but you're not sure what it was you did right. You can build on productive failures. You can't build on a non-productive success.

The more actions you take, the more productive failures you'll experience. The more productive failures you experience, the more you'll learn. Thomas Edison experienced 1,100 productive failures before he found the right filament for his incandescent lamp.

To turn your mistakes into learning opportunities, follow these suggestions:

A. *Have measurable goals.*
B. *Acquire a learning mentality.*
C. *Seek positive and negative feedback.*
D. *Develop a system for decision-making.*

MEASURABLE GOALS

You won't know whether you're moving toward your goals unless you have some way of measuring the motion. That's why your goals should be specific.

If your goal is to "learn photography," how will you know when you've reached it? When you've learned to aim the camera and press the shutter release? Your goal has to be more tangible than that:

"By July a year from now, I will have published my first photograph."

Now you have an easy way of determining whether you've reached your goal. If, by next July, one of your photographs has been published, you will have reached your goal. If none has been published, you didn't reach your goal.

If you haven't reached your goal, you'll want to ask why. You may determine that:

(a) Your photographic equipment is inadequate for the quality of photographs needed for publication. In that case, you should modify your action plan and take action to acquire the type of equipment you need.

(b) You've been submitting color photographs and the publication to which you've been submitting them uses only black-and-white. In that case, you must either switch to black-and-white photos or find a publication that uses color.

(c) Your photographs are technically good, but the composition does not meet the publication's standards. In that case, you'll need to upgrade your composition by seeking out a mentor, by reading literature on the subject or by studying the works of successful photographers and emulating them.

If you've reached your goal, you can press on to your next goal:

"By next year, I will have a full-time job as a photographer."

ACQUIRE A LEARNING MENTALITY

A learning mentality will help you create and acquire knowledge, share it with others, and use it to guide your behavior.

Learning can be divided into three categories:

(a) *Formal learning.*
(b) *Informal learning.*
(c) *Incidental learning.*

FORMAL LEARNING

Formal learning is the learning you acquire in a classroom or in seminars. In most settings, it's a passive type of learning. You listen while an instructor or facilitator provides you with information. You may need to pursue this type of learning to upgrade your knowledge in your field of endeavor. For instance, if you find yourself in need of more computer literacy, you may want to enroll in a community-college course to acquire this learning.

INFORMAL LEARNING

Informal learning is more active. You perceive the need to acquire certain knowledge, so you set out to acquire it. The learning is self-directed, and aimed toward achieving a purpose. Informal learning can be the most effective learning, because it can be directed explicitly toward the goals you are pursuing.

You can pursue informal learning in several ways;

(1) *Experimentation.* This is an excellent way to create knowledge. Through experimentation, you explore new methods and techniques. The budding photographer, for instance, might use different lenses, different filters and different exposure techniques to learn how to achieve unusual effects. The sculptor might experiment with different types of materials, the painter with different types of brush, the woodworker with different types of wood.

293

Experimentation might consist of a continuing series of minor projects designed to increase your knowledge a little at a time. Or it might consist of a pilot program to determine the feasibility of a major undertaking.

Experimentation should be carried out along the principles of the scientific method: accumulate data through observation and experimentation; form a hypothesis; test the hypothesis.

(2) *Personal Experience.* "Good judgment comes from experience," said Mark Twain. "And where does experience come from? Experience comes from bad judgment."

Once you've tried an ineffective solution to a problem, it becomes a valuable part of your experience. You know not to try that solution on that particular problem again.

Experience can also come from good judgments. When a problem arises as you move toward your goals, search your memory. Have you ever confronted a similar problem before? Did you solve it? If so, how did you do it?

In the corporate world, some of the more outstanding success stories were postscripts to poor judgments. Two researchers studied more than 150 new products during the '80s and found that a high percentage of them grew out of knowledge gained from previous failures. Among them was IBM's highly successful 360 computer series, which was based on the technology of an earlier computer that flopped.

(3) *Experience of others.* Sometimes you can avoid the pain of mistakes by profiting from the mistakes of others. You can also benefit from their successes. Look for others who have met the challenges you're facing. Find out how they overcame them, and what mistakes they committed along the way.

Look to others, also, for tips on what has worked for them. Adopt their techniques if they appear adaptable to your needs. In industry, this is known as benchmarking, and it has worked for some of the largest and most progressive companies in the world.

INCIDENTAL LEARNING

You acquire informal learning by deliberately and purposefully looking for the knowledge you need to attain your goals.

Incidental learning is acquired unconsciously. You acquire incidental learning as you go about performing your tasks.

The story of Pearl M. King and the "linking process" illustrates the difference between informal and incidental learning.

"Linking" was once part of the process of producing embroidered stockings. It was a difficult task to learn. Nine out of 10 newcomers quit before they mastered it. Those who did succeed usually required 18 to 36 months to achieve proficiency.

The steps in linking were known, but the subtle techniques that made the difference between a novice and a skilled worker were hard to pinpoint. The workers acquired these techniques unconsciously, through incidental learning, and were unable to tell anyone how they did it. A time-and-motion expert watched them at work and tried to develop a training program based on what he saw. But the program was a failure.

The factory finally hired King. She was asked to learn the linking task, then develop a way to teach it.

It took 26 days for her to acquire sufficient skill to perform the task slowly but accurately. In that time, she discovered the subtle clues that were not obvious to the visible observer. Purposeful informal learning enabled her to learn the techniques that the workers acquired through unconscious incidental learning. Then she was able to develop a formal training program to pass the techniques on to others more quickly and effectively.

Because it is unconscious, incidental learning can be misleading. We can make unconscious assumptions that, upon conscious examination, prove to be wrong. That's why it's important in problem-solving to examine the basic assumptions you make about a situation before proceeding toward a solution.

Sometimes, too, incidental learning teaches you the wrong techniques. These techniques become unproductive habits that must be unlearned before you move on to the next level of achievement.

SEEK POSITIVE AND NEGATIVE FEEDBACK

Once you've acted, you must evaluate the results of your actions. That's an important part of the learning process. But if you rely only on your own evaluation, you won't get a balanced view. You need feedback from others.

The more subjective the criteria for your success, the more you need feedback from others.

If you're looking for success in the photography field, some judgments will come easily. A picture is either in focus or it's not. It's usually obvious when the exposure is too light or too dark.

But you may find disagreement over whether you've taken the photo from the proper angle; whether you've posed your model gracefully or awkwardly; whether the total effect is dramatic or bland. For such judgments, it's best to seek feedback from others.

It's impossible to be completely objective about your own actions. When you cultivate a set of habits, you become attached to them and defensive about them. To admit that the habit is unproductive is to admit that you made a mistake, and nobody enjoys admitting to mistakes.

Others can see our actions more clearly. They can stand at arm's length and, often, discern even more clearly than you, where these actions are leading. Others may also have the advantage of experience to give them perspective.

So as you execute your action plan, stop at intervals to talk to others about what you're doing. If you're encountering obstacles, share them with friends, family and associates. Someone you know may have the perfect answer to your problem. Someone may make a dynamite suggestion that will help you achieve your goals more effectively. At the very least, you may pick up the germ of an idea that will provide the seed of success.

When you seek feedback, don't just go to the people you know will agree with you. Ask for comments from those you know will hold a different viewpoint. You don't have to be guided by the opposing view, but you should give it thoughtful consideration. It may suggest some modification that will improve your action plan.

Ask for specific feedback. If someone says "That's a great photograph," ask what makes it great. If someone says "This shot turns me off," probe to find out what the turn-off is. It may be a personal hang-up, or it may be some basic flaw that you need to correct.

When you ask for feedback, you have to be willing to expect negative criticism. Don't let it clobber your self-esteem. Unless you know what's wrong, you can't fix it.

But don't take all criticism at face value. Criticism springs from different motives. Some people may hold back negative criticism for fear of offending you and losing your friendship. Others may look only for the negatives, believing that by minimizing someone else's achievements they can make themselves look wiser or more successful.

When you hear negative criticism, consider the other's perspective. A 55-year-old woman has a different perspective from a 25-year-old man or an 18-year-old woman. A Ph.D. has a different perspective from someone with a high-school education. A millionaire has a different perspective from a wage-earner. One perspective may be no more valid than another, but you must learn to relate their perspectives to the actions they're evaluating. If you're designing a line of clothing for young people, don't scrap all your designs because your grandmother says she wouldn't be caught dead in them. You're not designing them for your grandmother. But if you ask your grandmother *why* she doesn't like the styles, she might come up with some objective observations that may indeed be valid. And if you're designing clothing for older persons, by all means pay attention to her immediate reaction.

If your action plan calls for hitchhiking across Europe to acquire an international perspective, your grandfather might think that outlandishly impractical. From his perspective, your time might be better spent acquiring experience and seniority in a position at home. But your grandfather grew up in a more stable business climate, where it was reasonable to expect to stay with the same company, on the same career track, for most of your working life. From the perspective of the turn of the 21st century, that may not be a reasonable prospect at all. A global perspective may be more important than a couple of years of experience. You'll have to make that decision in the light of your vision, your values, and your goals.

DEVELOP A DECISION-MAKING PROCESS

Haphazard decisions won't move you steadily toward your goals. You need a systematic method of arriving at decisions. Here is a six-step process based on one that was developed by The Xerox Corporation as part of its quality-improvement process:

1. *Identify the issue.*

2. *Analyze the issue.*

3. *Generate alternatives.*

4. *Select a specific alternative.*

5. *Implement the decision.*

6. *Evaluate the results.*

At each stage of the decision-making process, it helps to follow a process of expansion and convergence. What do we mean by that?

In the expansion phase, you lay all the possibilities on the table. In the convergence phase you narrow the possibilities down to a single option, which carries you to the next step.

Step 1: **IDENTIFY THE ISSUE**

Your first step is to decide what issues you should be addressing.

You have taken action. You either accomplished what you set out to accomplish, or you fell short. You must now decide what to do next. What worked the way it was supposed to work? What didn't work that needs to work?

First list all the issues you need to address if you're to move on to your next goal. Then narrow the list down to the issue that *must* be addressed before you can take the next step. Make that the next issue on your agenda.

Step 2: **ANALYZE THE ISSUE**

Now you need to look at the issue from all angles. Why is it necessary to make a decision on this issue? What will happen if you don't make it? What do you want to happen as a result of the decision? What stands in the way of making this happen? List the obstacles that must be overcome as a result of the decision. Then rank them in the order in which they must be overcome.

Step 3: GENERATE ALTERNATIVES

Take the obstacles one at a time and list possible ways to remove them. You can rely on your experience, the experience of others, and your imagination. Brainstorm the subject with others to provide you with a good inventory of alternatives. Make a short list of the alternatives you consider the most likely to work.

Step 4: SELECT A SPECIFIC ALTERNATIVE

Take the short list and decide which criteria you will use to select the best decision. Will it be the one that requires the least amount of time? The least amount of money? The least amount of effort? Analyze the alternatives in the light of your criteria, and choose the one that matches them the closest. Describe the actions you must take to implement the decision and the results you expect to accomplish as a result.

Step 5: IMPLEMENT THE DECISION

Execute the actions you described in Step four.

Step 6: EVALUATE THE RESULTS

After executing the decision, examine the results in the light of your expectations. Did the decision accomplish what you wanted it to accomplish? If so, mark it accomplished and move on to the next issue. If not, repeat the process, starting with Step 1: Identify the things you need to do to accomplish your objective and proceed.

If you follow these procedures, you will continually learn from your mistakes and build on your successes. Your path to your vision will be well marked and well illuminated. You will be able to observe and measure your progress, and savor the moment when your vision finally is realized.

Stairway To Success

Prelude to Step Six

After The End, The Beginning

The purpose of life after all is to live it, to taste the experience to the utmost, to reach out eagerly and without fear for newer and richer experiences.

—Eleanor Roosevelt

You've heard the expression "Getting there is half the fun." After an exciting trip to your dream vacation site, arrival can sometimes be a letdown.

It's true of life as well as of vacation trips. Alexander the Great had a vision of world conquest, and he achieved it within his own definition. At the height of his power, his empire extended into three continents. Standing astride the Mediterranean Sea, he controlled the civilized world from the valley of the Nile in Africa to the Hindu Kush on the borders of present-day India.

Yet, according to legend, Alexander wept because he had no more worlds to conquer.

Many people feel that way after they've achieved their visions. Many a couple forms a vision of a home, a career, and a family of happy, healthy children. Through hard work and ingenuity, they achieve everything they sought.

Then one day they realize that the home is paid for, the children are educated and have successful families of their own, their retirement nest egg is substantial and secure — and they have nothing left to live for.

The tragedy is that many such people equate the achievement of their vision with the end of their life's mission.

Nothing could be further from the truth.

Had Alexander expanded his perspective, he might have realized that beyond the eastern edge of his empire lay the riches of China and the Indies; across the Western ocean lay two immense undiscovered continents and yet another ocean.

He might also have discovered a large field for cultivation in his own back yard. As the master of such an immense stretch of territory, he had an unparalleled opportunity to exert moral leadership and to effect positive political and social change that could alter history irrevocably.

Look upon your vision that same way.

You have achieved what you set out to achieve. You've climbed your peak, and now you're standing on the summit. What do you see?

More peaks! Some may be loftier than the one you're on; no peak is so tall that it can't be a stepping-stone. Some may not be quite as lofty, but they're there, waiting to be climbed, and each represents challenges and rewards different from the one you just scaled.

That's why the sixth step on the stairway to success is "Recommitment." When you've fulfilled one vision, it's time to commit to another.

The poet T. S. Eliot once wrote:

> We must not cease from exploration, and the end of all exploring will be to arrive where we began and to know the place for the first time.

If you compare your life to that vacation trip, you can understand the poet's point. You work all year long for that vacation, putting aside the necessary money, going through the travel brochures, savoring the expectation of two weeks on the beach or in the midst of mountain splendor — and the exciting things you'll see and do en route to your destination.

The pleasure of the vacation is in the savoring as well as in the experiencing. As Stephen Covey has observed, "Satisfaction is a function of expectation as well as realization."[1]

The end of every vacation trip is the return home. Usually, no matter how much you enjoyed the vacation, your driveway is a welcome sight. You're glad to be home again, sleeping in your own bed, relaxing in familiar surroundings. You're seeing the everyday scene in a new and refreshing light.

You now begin a new cycle of work and saving and savoring that eventually will bring you to another vacation. Each cycle represents an ending and a renewal.

Look upon your life that way. The achievement of your vision is the rewarding vacation you've worked and planned for. Enjoy it. Celebrate it. Cherish the memory. But don't regard it as the end. Regard it as a new beginning.

The new beginning can take a number of forms.

The empty-nesters who worked so hard for a stable family, a good home and a secure retirement can now form a vision around their grandchildren. Or they can plan to travel, to cultivate new experiences or to devote themselves to worthy causes that capture their imagination. They might even envision new and stimulating careers.

ACHIEVEMENT BEYOND THE PRESIDENCY

Most Americans would regard the presidency as an incomparable pinnacle. Once you've won the White House, what else is there to achieve?

Yet many men who occupied that position created and followed new and rewarding visions.

After he left office, Thomas Jefferson founded the University of Virginia, designed its buildings, planned its curriculum, hired its staff and became its first rector.

John Quincy Adams left the presidency and entered the House of Representatives, where he pursued a long career that was in many ways more distinguished than his presidency.

William Howard Taft became the chief justice of the United States after he left the White House.

Herbert Hoover headed a commission charged with preventing the spread of starvation in Europe following World War II, and later led another commission that recommended important structural changes to the American government.

Jimmy Carter has devoted his post-White House years to various forms of human-service activities, including the provision of housing for the poor in many lands.

If these men could find fulfillment after the achievement of their most ambitious visions, so can you.

You can keep yourself in a constant state of renewal, if you keep these two pointers in mind:

- Gear your life to the concept of change.

- When you find yourself on a plateau, look for another level.

Chapter Eighteen

Gear Your Life to the Concept of Change

Getting off the tiger of change is not feasible.
Tiger-riding lessons are necessary. . .

— John D. Adams, Ph.D.

Abraham Lincoln once told of the Eastern monarch who challenged his wise men to invent a sentence that would be true and appropriate in all times and situations. They presented him with the words: "And this, too, shall pass away."

As the 20th century gives way to the 21st, these words become ever more appropriate. It is now a cliche to say that rapid change has become the norm.

The changes reach into the social, moral and spiritual dimensions of life, as Dr. Ernesto Michelucci, psychologist with the Rochester (N. Y.) Mental Health Center, has pointed out. Michellucci has counseled many people who found themselves jobless after massive layoffs at Eastman Kodak, Xerox and other large companies in the Rochester area.

He observed:

> *As a society, we are moving away from the idea of one marriage, one family, one career — but so many people here still hold on to that world view. I try to get across to them that the **zeitgeist**[2] is completely different today.*[3]

No one is immune from these changes, but when you focus your life on principles you can negotiate the changes more surely. People can be unreliable and disloyal; possessions can lose their value; jobs that once stimulated you can become boresome. But principles remain steady through it all.

As a laid-off corporate director of marketing and public relations told *__Fortune__*:

> *I don't think I will ever invest so much of myself in my job again. I defined myself by my job and the work relationships around me.*[4]

If you live by a set of principles that remain constant even through turbulent change, you will be able to deal more constructively with the change. You will maintain the power to choose the way you respond to situations. And you will be able to create

314

new situations by committing to new visions when the time comes to do so.

PREPARE FOR NEW WORLDS

Even as you follow your current vision, you can prepare yourself for the day when the vision is fulfilled and you must look for other worlds to conquer.

This is especially true when it comes to careers. It was once possible for young people to set their minds on a particular career in the confident expectation that they would be able to master it and grow prosperous in it by the time they reached middle age. They could expect to start work with a solid, substantial company, and work their way up through the hierarchy to secure, good-paying positions.

Today, notes ___Fortune___, many people with excellent technical educations "have discovered that their skills have peaked five years after graduation and that they will be replaced by more recent graduates."[5]

In such a fast-paced environment, success requires that you cultivate adaptability to change. So even as you pursue your present vision, acquire the qualities that will enable you to create and pursue subsequent visions that will be equally exciting.

AFTER-EFFECTS OF DOWNSIZING

The future holds much cause for optimism, but you must be prepared to deal with the circumstances of the future.

During the decade of the '90s, most large companies executed some form of downsizing, resulting in massive layoffs of middle-management as well as production workers.

The trend has been to target functions instead of people. But when new management or new technologies replace entire functions, the people who performed those functions are out of jobs, and their old skills are useless.

OLD SKILLS WON'T SUFFICE

The new economy will create many good jobs. But to take advantage of them, you'll have to acquire the education and the skills to perform them. The skills you used on the old job probably won't be enough.

For instance, Pacific Telesis Group (Pac Bell) used to dispatch 20,000 trucks a day to respond to calls from customers having problems with their lines. If the defect was inside the home or office, it was the customer's problem, and customers would usually elect to do the repairs themselves. PacBell developed an electronic system that would tell instantly whether the problem was in the domain of the company or the customer. If it was on the customer's side, no truck would be sent. An experiment with the new system in Santa Clara, Calif., resulted in a 30% reduction in the number of trucks dispatched.[6] The truck drivers who are replaced by this automation won't be able to get new jobs with PacBell driving trucks. They will need other skills.

HIGHER EDUCATIONAL REQUIREMENTS

New jobs are being created, but they require higher levels of education than the old jobs they replace. United Parcel Service, for example, increased its force of information-technology employees from 90 in 1983 to 3,000 in 1994. But the clerical and delivery personnel they replaced could not qualify for the new jobs without acquiring new skills.

When AT&T replaced 15,000 long-distance operators with automated equipment, the operators could not go out and get jobs as installers of wireless communications equipment — at least not without extensive retraining.

BROAD SKILLS AND PEOPLE SKILLS

Technical skills will be valuable in the future, if they are skills that can be applied in a broad variety of situations. Skills that are applicable only to a single job are vulnerable to advancing technology. If technology provides a new way to do the job, the skills become obsolete.

People skills, however, do not become obsolete. That's why it's important that you acquire leadership and interacting skills if you expect to get ahead. They will serve you well in a wide variety of organizations.

As the concept of teamwork and cooperation takes hold in organizations of all kinds, the ability to work with others becomes paramount. You'll need to be able to interact with others, provide leadership within team settings, communicate clearly and assertively, and be at home with computers. These skills can provide you with the flexibility to move into many different roles in many different organizations.

Anthony Patrick Carnevale, in his report, "America and the New Economy," expressed it this way.

> *As employees become more interdependent, the softer social skills become more important. The technical knowledge necessary to perform a task must be accompanied by the more complex capability for playing roles in the context of a group. The fundamental social skill is the ability to manage oneself. Self-esteem is the taproot to effective management, and self-loathing is the most fundamental impediment to successful interaction with others. Self-awareness is also critical to self-management. Employees need to understand their limits, ability to cope, and impact on others. The ability to set goals and motivate oneself to achieve is critical to being a team member; lack of motivation or goal-setting skills can create an undercurrent that can undermine team accomplishments.[7]*

TRENDS IN CAREER PATHS

Here are some of the changes in career opportunities as Carnevale sees them:

- ◆ *Brokers will replace bosses.* While the new economy will still need managers, professionals and service providers, their roles

318

will change. Instead of being bosses, they will be leaders, "easing transactions in internal and external networks, communicating new information and learning throughout networks, and leading and developing other employees."[8]

♦ *Technical specialists will replace less skilled labor.* Technical specialists include manufacturing engineers, health technologists, and, in banking, specialized bond traders. Computer and communications workers will grow in importance as business uses high-tech equipment to substitute for human brains and muscle. The manufacturing technician, aided by an array of technology, will be able to perform the work once carried out by manual laborers, material handlers, machine operators, repair workers, and even supervisors. Computers and advanced information systems will make it possible for one customer-service professional to do the work once delegated to lower-level clerical, sales and delivery people.

♦ *Manufacturing personnel will replace craft workers.* As businesses develop innovative ways to add value to raw materials, manufacturing processes will replace crafts-manship. Already boxed beef is making an end run around the local butcher. The housing industry, one of the last refuges for crafts workers, is beginning to shift toward manufactured components that are assembled on site.

♦ *Teams will replace individual professionals*. The trend is toward professional generalists, assisted by teams of technical specialists and paraprofessionals. Technicians, armed with flexible information technologies, are performing functions once performed by scientists and engineers. Professional bond specialists and currency experts are working with senior bank managers. Parapro-fessionals are showing up in medicine and law. The traditional classroom teacher's functions are now being carried out by master teachers, apprentice teachers, teachers' aides, and media specialists. In most settings, but not all, the generalist commands the highest income and the senior role.

♦ *People will become interchangeable from one industry to another*. Data processing experts, for instance, may move from a bank to an insurance company to a parts warehouse without having to undergo complete re-education. Those who prepare for this type of environment will find that they have considerable flexibility in charting their career paths.

♦ *Education will replace experience*. The "battlefield commissions" by which faithful workers used to advance through the ranks will be a thing of the past. No longer can a young person start in the lowliest job in the mail room and progress toward upper management through sheer loyalty and hard work. Increasingly, education will be the key to advancement.

This has been a jarring change for many corporate people. As ***Fortune*** reported:

For decades, until January 1988, a big New York bank promised workers that anyone with 20 years' experience would never be laid off... Says a human resources executive at the bank: "That was okay when we were clerically intensive and needed the mindset of a grunt. But as the organization changed in the Eighties and technology became important, we found that the people who came for security wouldn't adopt new ways of doing things."

THE ENTREPRENEURIAL MENTALITY

The new business environment means that negotiating the corporate ladder can be almost as tricky, and as risky, as following the entrepreneurial path.

In fact, businesses increasingly are seeking out people with entrepreneurial instincts. They are giving them a stake in corporate success while requiring them to share in corporate risks.

So whether your vision calls for growing your own company or working for someone else's company, you will need to develop the capacity to take intelligent, innovative risks.

You will also need to make education a continuing, neverending process.

Dream big dreams, plan for their fulfillment, act to implement your plan, and learn constantly.

Then, when the dream becomes real, dream another dream. Life goes on, and change is inevitable. Don't let it frighten you. Stay in control, and it will be change for the better.

Chapter Nineteen

Create a New Beginning

*Any time you stop striving to get better,
you're bound to get worse.*

—Pat Riley

Life should be an adventure, to be savored from beginning to end. It is a game of constantly changing odds, constantly developing challenges, constantly opening opportunities.

To win it, you have to play it. Sitting on the sidelines won't do. Even after you've achieved all you ever hoped to achieve, it's no time to stop living.

To live, you must have a purpose to guide you.

"Happiness," observed W. H. Sheldon, "is essentially a state of going somewhere wholeheartedly."

To go somewhere wholeheartedly, you must have your eye fixed on a destination that touches your passions.

In the preceding chapter, we touched on the changing social and economic climate, including the changing nature of the job market. To achieve success in this climate, you must regard the changes as challenges instead of threats.

AN ERA OF EXHILARATING OPPORTUNITY

Many people become frightened when they perceive the end of the stable career path that led steadily upward from diploma to gold watch.

Yet the future holds out for today's young people exhilarating opportunities that were not there for previous generations. People today have the opportunity to reinvent themselves, over and over, in exciting new roles. ***Fortune's*** Brian O'Reilly described the new relationship between employers and employees and observed: "If the old arrangement sounded like binding nuptial vows, the new one suggests a series of casual, thrilling — if often temporary — encounters."[1]

As the large crop of "baby boomers" moves into retirement, the job market will shift in favor of the work force, and people will have the option of working well into their retirement years, if they choose.

With today's longer life expectancies, even those who have spent lifetimes in the same career niche will be able to start new careers after 65, perhaps with less stress and more fulfillment than in their old careers.

FIVE TYPES OF TERRAIN

Regardless of whether you're over 60 or under 40, the achievement of your vision means that it's time for recommitment to a new and exciting vision.

The career path can lead to different types of terrain that can limit your upward mobility.

We'll discuss five of them here:

1. The box canyon.
2. The briar patch.
3. The badlands.
4. Green pastures.
5. The barnyard.

1. THE BOX CANYON

The *box canyon* is a familiar formation in organizations that still follow the top-down authoritarian management style. Most people are familiar with this land formation from Western movies. The trail leads into the canyon and dead-ends at a steep, sheer wall. There's no way up and no way around. The only way to go anywhere is to retrace your steps and leave the canyon.

In *box-canyon* organizations, room at the top is reserved for a limited few — usually no more than 1% of the work force. The unprivileged 99% are relegated to the role of taking orders from above and executing them the way they're told. They've encountered the walls of the *box canyon*, and there's nowhere for them to go except out the way they came.

You may have found a comfortable role in such an organization early in your career. You dreamed of becoming good at what you did. You formed your dream into a vision, you set goals and you drew up an action plan.

Now your vision has been achieved. You're a pro at what you do. Your peers look up to you. They recognize your skill, your loyalty and your good work habits.

You're earning a comfortable salary. But the job is no longer challenging. You want to move up.

But in *box canyon* organizations, loyalty, skill and hard work don't necessarily win you advancement. There's room at the top for only 1% of the people, and if the rooms are all taken, your loyalty, skill and hard work will buy you a cup of coffee in the company cafeteria, but not much else.

If you've achieved your vision and now find yourself in such an organization, you have two options: You can wait for the organization to change, or you can change organizations. You can create a new vision, commit yourself to achieving it, and take your loyalty, skills and work habits down a new path.

2. THE BRIAR PATCH

In Joel Chandler Harris' tales of Uncle Remus, the hero is a brash rabbit who is constantly outsmarting the fox. On one occasion, the fox catches the rabbit and is trying to dream up the most dreadful means of doing him in.

The rabbit pleads, "Don't throw me in the *briar patch.*"

The fox, believing that the rabbit is in terror of the *briar patch*, throws him in.

But the *briar patch*, of course, was the rabbit's home. He knew all the secret entrances and exits; all the hidden trails. He loved the challenge of hopping through the thorny passageways and outwitting his enemies. The rabbit wouldn't have left the *briar patch* if he could.

Many people feel that way about their niches in life. They find their jobs stimulating, their companions congenial, and their lifestyles satisfactory. They can find all the challenge they need right there in the *briar patch*.

If you're in such a situation, you don't have to abandon it for greener pastures just because somebody tells you things are better beyond the hedgerow. But you do need to stay prepared for changes.

Keep yourself constantly updated on developments in your field and in other fields that interest you. *Briar patches* don't last forever. Often they get cleared away for new developments. If that happens, you'll want to be prepared, and constant education is a good way to stay prepared. It's as true today as when a Greek philosopher named Aristotle first said it more than 2,000 years ago: "Education is the best provision for old age."

It's also the best provision for career crises.

3. THE BADLANDS

The *badlands* are hostile territory only to those who don't know how to cope with them. Those who are skilled in desert survival may find them challenging, stimulating and fascinating. Some organizational climates are like that. They may provide little support for the innovative risk-taker, but individuals may thrive on pet projects of their own. They act on their own initiative, despite the indifference of the organization. They get their ego satisfaction from the respect of their peers, often achieving recognition through professional and trade organizations. If you find yourself in such a situation, look ahead. Are you headed toward burnout? Can you continue to find fulfillment in your work despite the corporate attitude?

You may find that you can effect positive change within the organization by exerting leadership. Having achieved your vision so far as personal accomplishments are concerned, why not frame a vision for your team, department or other organization and commit yourself to making it a reality.

4. GREEN PASTURES

Many people reach career situations that seem to answer all their needs. They've worked their way into good positions with comfortable pay levels and responsibilities that don't stretch their abilities or their energies. They've found their *green pastures*. They don't need to look for better grazing, and they see no need to improve the grazing in their present pastures. They don't want more responsibility, they don't need more money, and they don't want to have to learn new things. They're happy and productive the way they are.

An organization that has too many happy people like that is in trouble. It won't innovate, it won't take risks, and it won't compete. In time, the *green pasture* may turn brown, or it may be overgrown with noxious weeds, and nobody will know how to deal with the crisis.

An individual with the *green pastures* mentality may also experience problems. Just as natural environments change, so corporate climates change. Remember that in the new economy, change has become a way of life. The comfortable behavior that once brought you all the rewards you wanted may soon become obsolete.

Pat Riley, the coach who made winners out of the Los Angeles Lakers and the New York Knicks, warns against the complacency that **green pastures** often engender:

There is a temptation to slack off when you feel good about what you've achieved — to let go of yesterday's hunger and insecurity and to accept the illusion that your struggle has ended.

Professional athletes know the dangers of complacency both in their professional and personal lives. Some reach their middle years and, when the adulation stops, settle into marginal careers. Some even hit bottom.

Those who survive are the ones who prepare for their post-glory days . . .[2]

You don't have to be a professional athlete to learn from Pat Riley. His words are valid for those pursuing non-athletic careers as well.

So never allow yourself to get too comfortable. Always keep your eye on the next move, the next change. Be prepared for it. Take the initiative in making it the kind of change you want, and not the kind of change you have to accept, like it or not.

5. THE BARNYARD

For some people, even **green pastures** are too challenging. They're like **barnyard** animals. They stand around waiting for whatever comes along. They watch idly as others take the initiative to better themselves and the organization. They're not interested in upgrading their skills, acquiring more education, or accepting more responsibility. They do what's expected of them, and no more.

Such people are unwilling to do the things that lead to success. If you're in that category, it's imperative that you begin immediately the six steps outlined in this book. Decide that you will do something meaningful with your life. Identify your talents, your values, and your preferred behavioral mode. Create a vision for a future in harmony with all those elements. Then set your goals, plan for their achievement, prepare for action — and act!

You will encounter similar terrain in your personal, social, spiritual and civic lives.

As you progress toward your vision in each of these areas of life, be aware of where you are — which goals you have achieved and which goals still lie ahead.

Be conscious of your terrain. Don't become so absorbed in the challenges of your **briar patch** that you lose sight of the challenges and opportunities that lie beyond it. Don't suffer burnout in the **badlands**. Don't be lulled into complacency by the comforts of **green pastures**, and don't let yourself be penned up in a **barnyard**.

As you see the approach of your vision's fulfillment, look upon it not as the end but as a new beginning.

Decide what you want to do with the next phase of your life, whether it be your life in retirement, the next round of progress in your career, or the launching of an entirely new career.

Create a new vision. Set new goals, and plan for their achievement. Then prepare for action — and act!

If you follow this process, you will find your life always stimulating and always challenging. And you will achieve success in its only meaningful definition: the definition that you yourself have written.

Stairway To Success

Chapter Twenty

Seize the Day!

Seize the day; put no trust in the morrow.
— Horace

You may be familiar with the quote from Horace in its Latin version, *Carpe diem*, made famous in the movie, ***The Dead Poets Society***, starring Robin Williams.

The ancient Roman was telling us that nothing gets done tomorrow. You have to act today if you expect to accomplish your purpose in life.

But while you must *act* today, you must keep your eye focused on tomorrow and the next year and the next decade. If your vision does not extend beyond today, then you will become mired in failure, because success in life cannot be achieved in a single day.

Bill Walsh, the National Football League Hall-of-Famer and Stanford University coach, put it very effectively:

> *Perhaps the secret to effective action lies in how you interpret the length of the "day" in* **Carpe Diem***. If it's a moment, or a day, you're cutting down on the odds for success. But if you recognize that in business as in sports (or all of life, for that matter), there's a "season" made up of several opportunities, those odds go up considerably.*[1]

But the opportunities are like baseball pitches: You have to swing at them if you expect to hit the ball out of the park.

So Walsh adds:

> *The key to success is reaching out, extending yourself, striking, and then, if you fail, bouncing back and doing it again — being so resourceful that finally when the moment comes again you won't hesitate.*[2]

Hesitation results from an uncertainty about where you want to go and what you want to do to get there.

To seize the day, you must have a purpose, a vision, a set of goals and a plan for reaching them. You must begin climbing the six steps on the stairway of success.

So let us review them with a view toward seizing the day:

Step 1: DECISION

Decide *today* that you will be in control of your life; that you will craft your own definition of success and will do whatever is necessary to achieve it.

Use *Figure 1-1* to identify your strongest talents. Then use the forms at the end of Chapter Two to identify your *congenial competencies*, your *compatible careers* and your *congenial roles*.

Have you forgotten what those terms mean? Here are the definitions:

A *congenial competency* is *an activity that allows you to use your best talents in an enjoyable and satisfying way*. Remember that you are most likely to succeed when you're doing something that you enjoy doing and that you do well.

A *compatible career* is *a line of work that allows you to use your congenial competencies in a profitable way*.

A *congenial role* is *a position within a compatible career that lets you follow your normal behavior pattern most of the time*.

Your normal behavior pattern refers to your preferred way of responding to people and events in your life. Generally, people respond in four basic modes, one of which they prefer in most situations..

Those modes are:

Top Gun: The dominant, take-charge type whose chief motivation is to win. *Top Guns* make excellent leaders and long-range planners, but are often short on diplomacy. They believe in stating their wishes directly, and they relate to tasks more than to people.

Engaging: The friendly, sociable type whose chief motivation is to be admired. *Engagers* are excellent at organizing and motivating people. They are adventurous and fun-loving. They believe in stating their wishes directly, and they relate to people more than to tasks.

Accommodating: The steady, reliable type whose chief motivation is to be liked. *Accommodators* relate well to those who follow the other behavioral modes. They make excellent mentors. They prize security and dislike conflict. They believe in stating their wishes indirectly, through hints and suggestions. They relate to people more than to tasks.

Meticulous: The logical, pragmatic type whose chief motivation is to do things correctly. They excel at problem solving. **Meticulous** people strive to meet their own inner standards. They soak up information and are excellent at making sense out of complex data. They enjoy working alone. They tend to state their wishes indirectly, and relate to tasks more than to people.

Determine which of those descriptions most closely fits your behavior, and look for activities that will allow you to follow your preferred mode prof-

338

itably while doing the things you do well and enjoy doing.

Next, decide what values mean the most in your life, and develop a set of principles in support of those values. Then decide on the rules of conduct that will support these principles.

Again, let's define our terms:

A *value* is something you hold dear.

A ***principle*** is a broad, fundamental truth.

A ***rule of conduct*** is a guide to behavior designed to implement a principle.

List the things you value in each area of your life: your family, your career, your social life, your civic life and your spiritual life. Then decide what principles support these values and which rules of conduct you will follow to support these principles.

For instance, in your family life you may value family closeness. You may develop these principles in support of family closeness:

♦ Mutually enjoyable activities promote family closeness.

♦ Good communication is essential to family closeness.

You may then frame these rules of conduct for yourself:

- Each day I will do something enjoyable with my family.

- I will share my hopes and dreams and my challenges with my family, and will create a non-threatening environment in which they can come to me with their hopes, dreams and challenges.

Based on the values you have identified, decide what principles you will place at the center of your life. Use them as guidelines for all the decisions you must make.

Identify the areas of your life that concern you, and perform *situational triage*. Divide the situations that confront you into these categories:

(1) Those you want to influence and can.
(2) Those you'd like to influence but can't.
(3) Those that are not worth influencing.

Focus your efforts on those situations in the first category. Develop strategies for dealing with those in the second category. Don't waste your time on situations in the third category.

Step 2: COMMITMENT

To seize the day, you have to make an irrevocable commitment to act. You do this by wiping the slate clean, creating a new script, and embarking on a course from which there is no turning back. What's past is past; what's done is done. The important thing is what you can do *now* to achieve the future you want. This requires a willingness not only to accept change, but to *pursue it proactively*.

You now have a set of values supported by firm principles, and you have developed your own rules of conduct in support of those principles. You know where you want to focus your efforts to achieve the future you desire.

Now you must *create the future.* You do this by picturing in your mind the future as you want to see it. Mentally experience the sights, sounds, feelings, tastes and smells of the environment in which you choose to live. Create a future that will excite you and that will be in harmony with your deeply held values.

After you have created your vision, describe the future you desire in a written mission statement. This will serve as a constant reminder of what you have determined to accomplish.

After you've created your future, cross your Rubicon. This means, commit to a course of action from which there is no turning back. Unless you are willing to commit yourself totally to your vision, your resolution will fail at the first sign of adversity. Cross the river and burn your bridges.

Step 3: PLANNING

You now have a vision and a mission statement that describes the future you have created. Your next step is to plan to turn the vision into reality.

Your plan should specify the actions you must take to realize your vision. It must set a timetable for taking each action. And it must be flexible enough to allow for course corrections along the way.

To plan effectively you'll need to do these three things:

1. Set goals.
2. Set priorities.
3. Develop strategies.

You begin by breaking the mission into doable segments. Let these be your goals. Set long-term, intermediate-term, short-term and immediate goals, including the goals you must attain immediately if you are to embark toward your vision. Start with the vision and plan back to the present. Do this for every aspect of your life.

Set measurable goals, so that you'll know for sure when you've attained them. Advertise them. When you know that others are aware of your goals, you'll have extra incentive to reach them.

You set priorities by listing the situations that you have decided to influence after performing *situational triage*. You then evaluate these situations, asking yourself, "What is most important?" and "What is most urgent?"

Important choices move you toward your goals. *Urgent* choices demand immediate attention. Good planning involves reducing urgent choices to a minimum and concentrating on important choices. List these choices in the order of importance and address them one at a time.

After you have set your priorities, develop strategies for reaching your goals.

Strategies should specify the actions to be taken, the people who are to execute them, and the time frame in which they are to be executed. They should set deadlines for completion, and establish criteria for determining when the actions have been completed.

Step 4: PREPARATION

Success requires preparation. You must get ready to march toward your vision by acquiring balance in your physical, mental/emotional, social and spiritual lives. Physical health requires a good balance between work and recreation, exercise and rest, sleep and wakefulness. It also requires a balanced diet.

Mental/emotional balance requires that you recognize and appreciate your own self-worth while respecting the worth of others. It means learning to deal with the ups and downs of life without being thrown off balance. It requires that you learn patience and forgiveness and acquire a sense of humor. It means taking charge of your own life and accepting responsibility for your successes and failures.

Social balance enables you to become a participating member of society. It means cultivating a supportive circle of friends in your family, your work place, your community, and your leisure activities.

Spiritual balance requires that you get in touch with your core values — the things that make you who and what you are. Spiritual values transcend the material artifacts that we can touch and see. They take us into the realm of beauty, inspiration, and love. Material success may result in the accumulation of possessions. But only spiritual success will enable you to enjoy them.

After you get ready through acquiring balance, you must get set by acquiring motivation and minimizing the restraining effects of stress.

You can boost your morale by cultivating sources of morale-boosting endorphins — substances secreted by your body which reduce pain and tension and give you an overall good feeling. Family closeness, involvement in worthy causes, relationships with supportive groups and vigorous exercise can all cause your body to produce more endorphins.

You can give yourself positive stress by accepting an exciting challenge, by upgrading your estimate of your own capabilities, and by following the doctrine of *and then some*. When you follow this doctrine, you give a challenge everything you've got, *and then some*.

Pain and pleasure can also provide positive stress. When the pain of staying in a rut is greater than the pain of getting out, you will make a positive change. When the rewards of getting out of the rut are appreciably greater than the rewards of staying in it, you will also make a positive change.

You can let pride and fear be positive motivators. You succeed because you don't want to experience the pain or the humiliation of failure.

You can also acquire positive stress by giving yourself a stake in the outcome. Whether your investment in an endeavor is monetary or emotional, your investment will give you an incentive to succeed.

Managing negative stress means dealing with the frustrations that arise when our bodies build up energy to confront a challenge and are unable to use it in constructive ways.

One of the best remedies for negative stress is action. You feel stressed out when you are not in control of events. Your stress diminishes when you can see that your actions are helping you gain control.

Honesty is another good antidote to stress. When you're being yourself, you don't have to deal with the constant fear that you'll be "found out."

Good exercise, a balanced diet, and a supportive network of friends are also helpful in managing stress.

Step Five: EXECUTION

Executing your strategies for success requires a spiral movement: First you act. Then you learn from your actions. Next you apply what you've learned through further action. Then you learn from your action and once more apply what you've learned. You continue the spiral until you have achieved your goal.

Action requires that you assemble your physical, financial and human resources, then begin executing your strategies one by one, always asking yourself, "What needs to happen next if I am to reach my goal?"

We learn through productive failures. In a productive failure, you don't achieve your objective, but you come away with new knowledge and understanding that will increase your chances of success on the next try.

To learn from mistakes, you need measurable goals and a learning mentality. A learning mentality means that you are alert for every opportunity to learn something new and useful, whether through formal courses or purposeful learning by doing.

You must also seek positive and negative feedback, and develop a system for decision-making.

Step 6: RECOMMITMENT

Achieving your vision doesn't mean you've reached the end of the line. It simply means that you've come to a new starting place. Once your desired future has become your happy present, look around for other visions to create. The future is still in front of you, and you can either accept whatever fate throws your way or you can once more create the future you want.

For the foreseeable future, you will be living in a world whose dominant characteristic is change. To be successful, you must learn to change with the world. By gearing your life to the concept of change, you can create a personal vision that enables you to ride the changes to the future you desire.

Most people, at one time or another in their lives, find themselves in an environment that seems to confine them to their current level of achievement. They may be content to remain in that environment, but the era of change makes that a hazardous choice: the environment is subject to change or even to destruction.

When you think you've reached the point at which you can stop all forward progress and stand pat for the duration, you're in danger.

Look about you for another exciting challenge. Form a new vision, and commit once more to its fulfillment.

When you do that, you will create for yourself a future of never-ending challenge, achievement, and excitement.

May the future you create exceed your fondest expectations!

END NOTES

Chapter I

1   Howard Gardner, <u>Frames of Man</u>, <u>The Theory of Multiple Intelligences</u>, (New York: Basic Books, Inc., 1983), pp. 73-276.

Chapter III

1   The Holy Bible, American Standard Version, 2 Timothy 3:5

2   Georgea Kovanis, "In Our Twenties," <u>The Detroit Free Press,</u> April 14, 1993, p.1J.

Chapter IV

1   Suzanne Chazin, "Give Yourself the Winning Edge," <u>Reader's Digest</u>, August 1993, p. 164.

2   John Pekkanen, "Drive of a Champion," <u>Reader's Digest</u>, August 1993, pp. 91-96.

Chapter VII

1   Tracy Goss, Richard Pascale, and Anthony Athos, "The Reinvention Roller Coaster: Risking the Present for a Powerful Future," <u>Harvard Business Review</u>, Nov.-Dec. 1993.

2   Louis S. Richman, "How To Get Ahead In America," <u>Fortune</u>, May 16, 1944, p. 47.

3   Richman, p.50.

4   Pat Riley, <u>The Winner Within, a Life Plan for Team Players</u>, (New York: G.P. Putnam's Sons, 1993).

Chapter XIII

1   Mary Baechler, "Death of a Marriage", <u>INC</u>., April 1994, p.74.

2   Harriet Webster, "Most Important Hour in a Child's Day," <u>Reader's Digest</u>, August 1993, p. 88.

3   Suzanne Chazin, "Give Yourself the Winning Edge," <u>Reader's Digest</u>, August 1993, pp. 165-166.

4   Brian O'Reilly, "Reengineering the MBA," <u>Fortune</u>, January 24, 1994, p. 40.

5   Brian O'Reilly, "Reengineering the MBA," <u>Fortune</u>, January 24, 1994, p.42.

Chapter XIV

1   Frank Rose, "A New Age for Business?," <u>Fortune</u>, October 8, 1990.

2   Lynne V. Cheney, "Points to Ponder," <u>Reader's Digest</u>, June 1993, p. 146.

Chapter XVIII

1   Stephen Covey, <u>The 7 Habits of Highly Effective People</u>, (New York: Simon & Schuster, 1989), p. 150.

2   Zeitgeist is a German word meaning the general trend of culture and taste during a particular era.

3   Susan Caminiti, "What Happens to Laid-Off Managers," <u>Fortune</u>, June 13, 1994, p. 69.

4   Brian O'Reilly, "What Companies and Employees Owe One Another," <u>Fortune</u>, June 13, 1994, p. 78.

5   Brian O'Reilly, "What Companies and Employees Owe One Another," <u>Fortune</u>, June 13, 1994, p. 50.

6   Joan E. Rigdon, "Retooling Lives: Technological Gains Are Cutting Costs, And Jobs, in Services," <u>The Wall Street Journal</u>, Feb. 24, 1994, p. A1.

7   Anthony Patrick Carnevale, <u>America and the New Economy</u> (American Society for Training and Development and the U.S. Department of Labor, Employment and Training Administration, 1991), p. 104.

8   Carnevale, p. 91.

Chapter XIX

1 Brian O'Reilly, "What Companies and Employees Owe One Another," Fortune, June 13, 1994, pp. 44-45.

2 Pat Riley, The Winner Within, a Life Plan for Team Players, (New York: G.P. Putnam's Sons, 1993).

Chapter XX

1 Bill Walsh, "Carpe Diem — Or the Diem After That," Forbes ASAP, Oct. 25, 1993, p. 17.

2 Ibid.

For information on Nido Qubein's speeches, books, cassettes and consulting, call or write:

Creative Services, Inc.
806 Westchester Drive
P.O. Box 6008
High Point, NC 27262 USA
Phone (336) 889-3010
Fax (336) 885-3001
www.NidoQubein.com